CHICANO GRAFFITI AND MURALS

Also in this series

The Holiday Yards of Florencio Morales: "El Hombre de las Banderas" by Amy V. Kitchener

Santería Garments and Altars: Speaking without a Voice by Ysamur Flores Peña and Roberta J. Evanchuk

Punk and Neo-Tribal Body Art by Daniel Wojcik

Chainsaw Sculptor: The Art of J. Chester "Skip" Armstrong by Sharon R. Sherman

Sew to Speak: The Fabric Art of Mary Milne by Linda Pershing

Vietnam Remembered: The Folk Art of Marine Combat Veteran Michael D. Cousino, Sr. by Varick A. Chittenden

Earl's Art Shop: Building Art with Earl Simmons by Stephen Flinn Young and D.C. Young

Chicano Graffiti and Murals: The Neighborhood Art of Peter Quezada by Sojin Kim

Folk Art and Artists Series
Michael Owen Jones
General Editor

Books in this series focus on the work of informally trained or self-taught artists rooted in regional, occupational, ethnic, racial, or gender-specific traditions. Authors explore the influence of artists' experiences and aesthetic values upon the art they create, the process of creation, and the cultural traditions that served as inspiration or personal resource. The wide range of art forms featured in this series reveals the importance of aesthetic expression in our daily lives and gives striking testimony to the richness and vitality of art and tradition in the modern world.

CHICANO GRAFFITI AND MURALS

THE NEIGHBORHOOD ART OF PETER QUEZADA

Sojin Kim

University Press of Mississippi Jackson

Photo and Illustration Credits: Somi Kim, p. 7, p. 21; Alan Thewles, p. 16; Michelle Quezada, p. 49, p. 55, plate 4, plate 5, plate 12, plate 13; Peter Quezada, p. 25, p. 26, p. 42, plate 3, plate 14; all other photos by Sojin Kim.

Manufactured in Hong Kong
98 97 96 95 4 3 2 1

Library of Congress Cataloging-in-Publication Data

Kim, Sojin.
Chicano graffiti and murals : the neighborhood art of Peter Quezada / Sojin Kim.
p. cm. — (Folk art and artists series)
Includes bibliographical references.
ISBN 0-87805-824-9 (cloth : alk. paper). — ISBN 0-87805-825-7 (pbk. : alk. paper)
1. Quezada, Peter—Criticism and interpretation. 2. Mural painting and decoration—20th century—California—Los Angeles. 3. Street art—California—Los Angeles. I. Quezada, Peter. II. Title. III. Series.
ND237.Q44K54 1995
759.13—dc20 95-22365
CIP

British Cataloging-in-Publication data available

In memory of Robert Michael Heisley, a dedicated and creative scholar of Folklore and Chicano Studies

CONTENTS

PREFACE

THIS MONOGRAPH describes the work of Peter Quezada. Quezada is a self-taught muralist who, for almost a decade, has prolifically painted his murals and lettering on buildings and retaining walls in neighborhoods that lie northeast of downtown Los Angeles. Quezada emphasizes that he began painting murals for "practical" purposes as opposed to "artistic" ones. He refers to his work as a "graffiti-deterrent" or a "substitute for graffiti," and he specifically selects as his sites those surfaces that are repeatedly marked by taggers and gang graffiti writers.

Often enlisting the assistance of taggers or gang members, Quezada designs his murals to appeal to these youth as well as to discourage them from participating in behavior he perceives as destructive: graffiti writing, drug use, and gang involvement. Many of his murals consist of text that explicitly implores with such messages as "Peace Brothers, It's Thee [sic] Only Way If We Are To Survive"; "End The Insanity. Have the Courage to Say No To Gangs"; "Drinking & Drugs Are Not Magic. Don't Do 'Em" (plates 5, 7, 12). Whether memorializing people he has known who have been killed in gang violence or painting business signage on commission, he designs his work stylistically and graphically to appeal to those who otherwise would be inscribing their names or the names of their gangs on the walls.

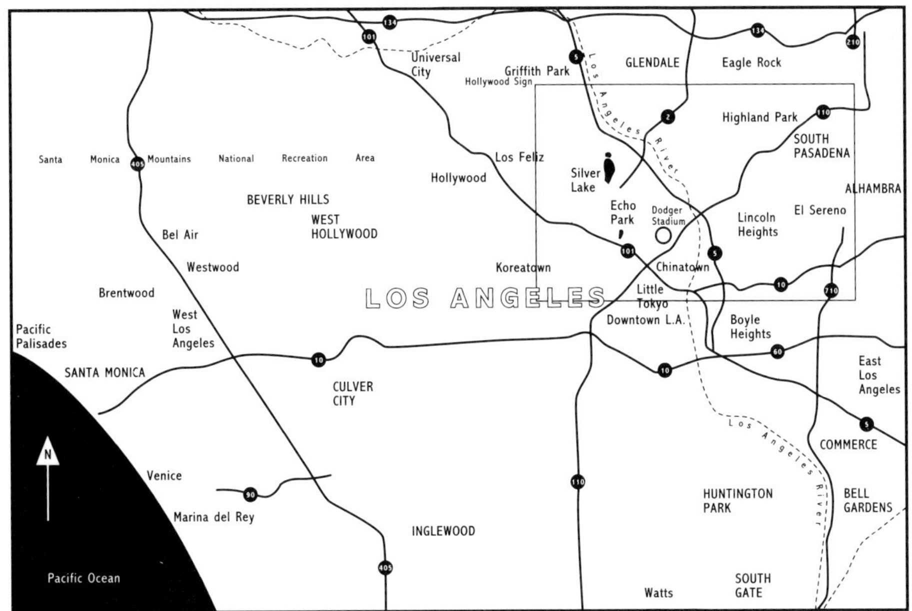

Map of Los Angeles.

This discussion of Quezada's work explores the artist's practical and aesthetic project, addressing the issues that prompted him to begin painting and the factors that inform his visual repertoire. His work will be considered against both a broad background of public arts movements in the United States and the more specific experiences and sentiments that powerfully connect individuals to the idea of "neighborhood." Neighborhoods are not simply geographic units organized according to municipal design; they are also social, emotional, and stylistic environments. At the same time, while all individuals find themselves associated with groupings of people based on geographic proximity, economic class, ethnic classification, and social affiliations, all of us are involuntary participants in mass-generated culture. This monograph explores the interplay among contemporary urban life, the mass-mediated images with which we are daily inundated, and physical space. It illustrates how an individual expresses the intangible aspects of his community and personal life in the physical, built environment.

While I sometimes refer to currents in Chicano visual art as it emerged in the late 1960s and early 1970s, I am hesitant to situate Quezada's work in this context. For one thing, Quezada himself does not cite these projects as a direct influence on his work. Second, the particularity of his personal aesthetics and preferences should

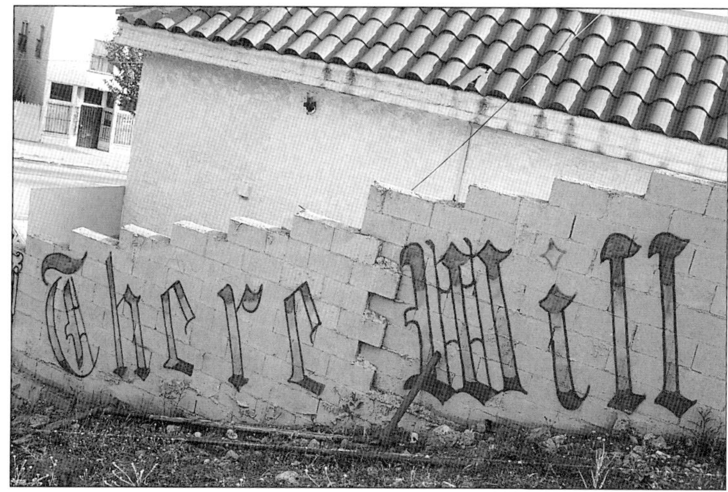

not be overlooked. And third, to place his work under the rubric of Chicano art seems to play into a popular perception that graffiti and murals are the inherent artistic domain of people of Mexican descent. I am reminded of the experience of an artist I met recently in Los Angeles. He is from Mexico, but he received his M.F.A. in California. Several years ago while he was traveling in Ireland, a group of young nationalistic artists enlisted his direction in a mural project. Although he is a photographer and filmmaker, they had assumed that because he was from Mexico —the country of Orozco, Siqueiros, and Rivera—he had some natural inclination for painting on walls.

Mural painting is not Quezada's vocation. Nor did he grow up feeling any sort of artistic calling. Nevertheless, I can-

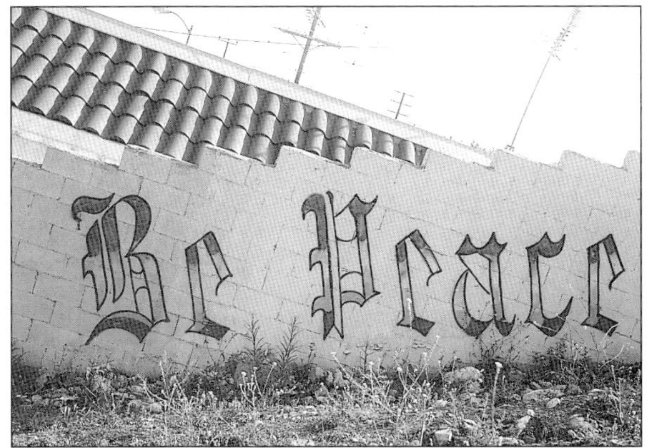

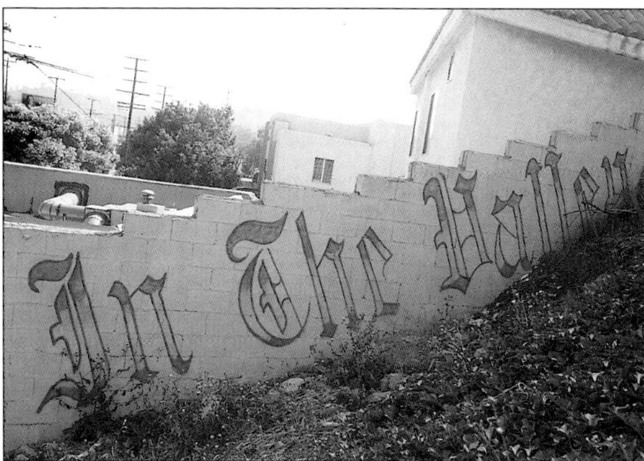

not dismiss the wide-reaching influence of the work produced by the idealistic and activist-minded Chicano artists of the 1960s and 1970s, and therefore I occasionally discuss Quezada's work in relation to *el movimiento*.

I had thought the palimpsest to be an apt metaphor for the way in which I researched and wrote this monograph. The term refers to writing surfaces reused multiple times; during the medieval period, scarcity of parchment paper necessitated that writing be scraped off existing pages to make room for new text. (Quezada's project lends itself well to this model; he covers up the existing writing on walls and reinscribes their surfaces with his messages.) My project of writing about Quezada and his murals has necessitated my acceptance of a process of rework, rewrite, and reconsider. Periodically I have had to scrape away at my misconceptions and misinterpretations in regard to Quezada's work:

SK: Where do you get the ideas for your words?

PQ: It's the stuff that I think is going to fly. Stuff that I think will last—will reach a broad audience without offending the ones that I'm targeting, which are the graffiti writers and gang members.

SK: There's a lot of reference in them to religious texts, right?

PQ: Some of it, yeah. Some of it's unintentional, though, really. Like the one that says "There will be Peace in the Valley" and then "And the Lion Shall Lay Down with the Lamb, Oh Lord." That's part of this song that Elvis did—Elvis sings it along with several other artists.

(scrape) (scrape) (scrape)

SK: How about the way you use "Thee" instead of "the"?

PQ: That one is kind of the religious thing. Well, actually, I use it because it's more the way it sounds when you speak: thee versus the. "Peace brothers, It's the [pronounced "thə"] only way . . . ," that doesn't sound the same as "Peace brothers, it's thee only way . . . " See, so a lot of it is just the way it sounds.

(scrape) (scrape)

Eventually, I realized that I took the metaphor of the palimpsest too literally. In fact, I began to notice that the concept was often employed in the writings of art critics and historians to imply the simultaneous existence of and inter-reference between the multiple voices that inform any cultural production. I decided that these layers of discovery could not be scraped away and dismissed so efficiently; multiple motivations can inform any one act or choice. Quezada himself, of course, is aware of the flexibility of meanings ascribed to his messages and imagery.

The discussion that follows does not resemble the order of my discoveries or inquiries. Just as Quezada picks through his reservoir of potential sources to create his murals, I selected pieces of information I have accumulated over the past two years to create this account of his work.

Accordingly, I acknowledge first Peter Quezada for being patient and forthcoming with me as I wrote and for the good will with which he paints his murals. I acknowledge as well the insights of Michelle Quezada and the technical assistance of Somi Kim, Dan T. Knapp, and Phillip McAbee. I am extremely grateful for the advice, suggestions, and editorial assistance of Michael Owen Jones, Somi Kim, and R. Mark Livengood.

CHICANO GRAFFITI AND MURALS

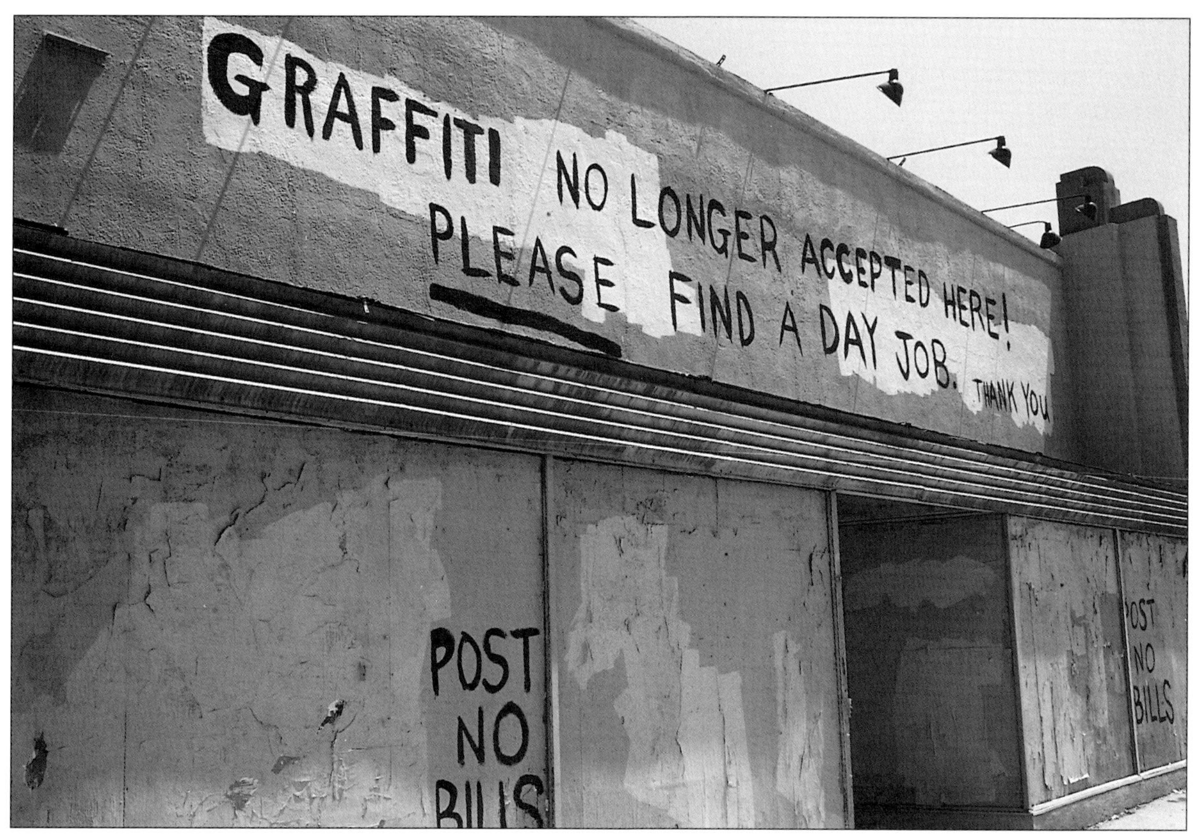

Anti-graffiti graffiti.

The Project

The walls that urban residents daily encounter are not merely structures containing and dividing space; they are also surfaces that become inscribed with different messages, which are read both figuratively and literally. The imperatives of many different groups contend and collude on these walls. Businesses create signage that will attract and inform customers of their services; marketing researchers determine which walls are located in areas with dense traffic, and advertisers pay big money to install their billboards in these prime spots; graffiti writers announce their presence and preeminence; and painters of murals enliven and transform otherwise nondescript surfaces in the public view. The language, size, and imagery of these messages are regulated by laws and upheld and enforced by citizens' groups. The condition and appearance of the built environment in any given area becomes its public face, its facade, its most immediate aspect. The appearance of a neighborhood's walls can affect an area's reputation, property values, and business—the general condition of life for those who live there.

Periodically these issues are argued publicly. For instance, English-speaking residents may object to the posting of business signage in non-English languages. The neighbors of popular singer Madonna recently complained that the exterior paint job on her new home was an eyesore. It is graffiti, however, that continually raises the ire of city residents. In 1993, the *Los Angeles Times* reported that, according to some sources, the county's annual spending on graffiti removal exceeded $100 million. Graffiti is implicated as an immediate indication of urban blight and crime in an area, and it is commonly discussed with words evocative of war, combat, or contagion. Various ordinances and fines have been instituted to curb graffiti. Several organizations and programs have developed mural programs as a strategy for replacing and discouraging graffiti on walls.

Peter Quezada undertakes his particular mural painting project in accordance with the latter objective. He indicates the criteria for the walls he selects for his murals: "The walls that I choose, they're graffiti-covered and for the most part they're no man's walls—retaining walls that are on abandoned property. So the walls that I take are sort of like orphan walls—walls that have been deserted by their real owners, or they actually belong to somebody but they're not taken care of graffiti-wise. They are walls that have been hit up by graffiti for a long period of time or they get hit up, as soon as they take it off it comes back. It comes off, they hit it up. It's just a cycle."

Much of the popular attention to graffiti has focused on New York City. The forms and styles developed in the 1970s by graffiti writers in New York received a great deal of media attention and subsequently spread to other metropolitan areas. "Tags" or "tagging" are the most prevalent and pesky forms of graffiti. An individual who went by the name of TAKI 183 became the first tagger of renown after writing his moniker on walls all over New York City in the late 1960s and early 1970s. Tagging refers specifically to the idiosyncratic stylized signatures of individual graffiti writers. The objective of taggers is to leave their mark in as many and as unlikely places as possible, demonstrating their ingenuity and mobility. "Pieces," short for masterpieces, are the larger, more intricately designed projects.

Before the emergence of New York-style graffiti and tagging in Los Angeles, Chicano youth in Southern California had developed their own distinctive styles for writing their names or the names of their gangs. These writings were referred to as *placas* or *plaqueasos*. Jerry and Sally Romotsky coined the term "Barrio Calligraphy" in the early 1970s when they surveyed graffiti in Chicano neighborhoods in Los Angeles. After talking with the writers, the Romotskys identified three distinct alphabet styles then in use: Point, Block, and Loop.

Quezada initially did not paint murals over the graffiti he was whitewashing. He did not seriously undertake artistic solutions to graffiti until 1986, when he began to teach himself to draw. He indicates that it was, in fact, the advent of taggers to Los Angeles that finally motivated him to make these efforts: "Taggers did tenfold the amount of damage on the walls than gangs had been doing. Walls that had been hit up by gangs and then had been painted over by myself and gangs were being hit up by taggers. It's a much harder thing to deal with than just looking for the gangs who did the graffiti and getting them to help fix up the walls and convincing them that the graffiti was ugly. Taggers just want to be up. There's no rhyme or reason to them."

Quezada's project is not unprecedented. A number of organizations nationwide have developed and sought with varying degrees of success to involve potential and practicing graffiti writers in mural projects or other "constructive outlets." Two examples are the Graffiti Alternatives Workshop, established in Philadelphia in 1970, and United Graffiti Artists, established in New York in 1972. All of these efforts may be considered as outgrowths of the broader public arts movement of the 1960s and 1970s.

In the late 1960s, artists in several major cities sought to make their work more socially relevant and immediate to the lives of the "community." By "community," these artists were referring to neighborhoods or groups of people that had traditionally been underserved by the arts establishment. Influenced by concurrent movements for civil rights and social justice, many artists considered murals to be a powerful vehicle for social change and empowerment. Sometimes called the "mural renaissance" or "the new mural movement," these public art activities were inspired in part by the educational murals commissioned by the Mexican government following the Revolution of 1910 and then by the United States government under the Works Progress Administration (WPA) in the 1930s. Artists collaborated with individuals in neighborhoods to produce murals with topical themes and images drawn from daily life. Through the project (the mural) and the process (work with the community and, in particular, inner city youth), artists became involved in urban renewal, community organizing, and education.

A prolific force in this mural renaissance were artists and individuals of Mexican descent, who identified themselves as Chicanos to indicate their political consciousness. From 1965, Chicanos were involved in a relatively cohesive effort for advances in their civil rights. Referred to as *el movimiento* or *la causa,* these efforts sought improvements in education, work conditions, and political representation. Central to these efforts was the assertion of Chicano identity in ways that would convey cultural dignity according to their own terms, sensibilities, and history. Chicano artists were instrumental in the dissemination of visual presentations of this empowerment. These artists deliberately selected and elevated specific aspects of Mexican history and culture as a means of countering the negative stereotypes. In order to recognize the everyday expressive life of the entire community, images and styles were drawn from religion, traditional folk arts, and vernacular graphics, as well as from the creative expressions of youth, gang, and prison cultures.

In Los Angeles, much of the Chicano public art created during the early 1970s involved the participation of graffiti writers and gang members in the designing and execution of murals. Murals were painted deliberately where graffiti had been, sometimes even incorporating graffiti into the style or design of the work. Quite a few murals dealt with gang violence and problems. Some of the major locally based organizations that grew out of these efforts in Los Angeles were Mechicano Art Center (1971), Citywide Mural Project (1974), East Los Streetscapers (1975), and the Social and Public Arts Resource Center (1976).

Peter Quezada's efforts are informed by many of the same concerns as these organizations, but he indicates that it was not explicitly on the model of graffiti arts or mural arts community collectives that he undertook his own mural projects. During the 1970s he had not been connected to the arts activities of *el movimiento;* much of the mural painting seems to have been in East Los Angeles, and Quezada does not recall any community murals being painted in the Echo Park neighborhood where he lived until the mid-1970s.

Quezada indicates that in fact he had not even been interested in art when he was growing up. In 1976, after he finished high school and spent a year attending Los Angeles City College, he moved to Highland Park in northeast Los Angeles. He went to work at Security Pacific Bank and also became friends with many of the youth who were in the gangs loosely organized around the numbered avenues that intersect the area. Quezada worked at Security Pacific Bank for ten years, from 1976 to 1986. In 1979, he informally began to council the youth he knew about alternatives to gang involvement, and he became concerned with the growing visibility of graffiti in the neighborhood. Using his own resources, Quezada started buying paint and going out to different sites in the area—initially simply whitewashing the graffiti, and then later painting murals. Making use of the trust and social acquaintances he had established among area gang members, he often convinced those who had done the graffiti to assist him in cleaning it up.

In 1986, Quezada left his job at the bank when he was offered a position as a full-time youth counselor with Community Youth Gang Services (CYGS). CYGS, one of the nation's largest anti-gang agencies, is a program run by Los Angeles County. Heralded as being effective and dedicated, it has also been criticized for its controversial use of counselors who have backgrounds of gang affiliation. While still at CYGS, Quezada began to paint murals in his neighborhood under the auspices of what he was calling "Neighborhoods for Peace Youth Program." When funding ran out for his position at CYGS, he incorporated Neighborhoods for Peace and continued his work with "at-risk youth." When lack of funding brought about the

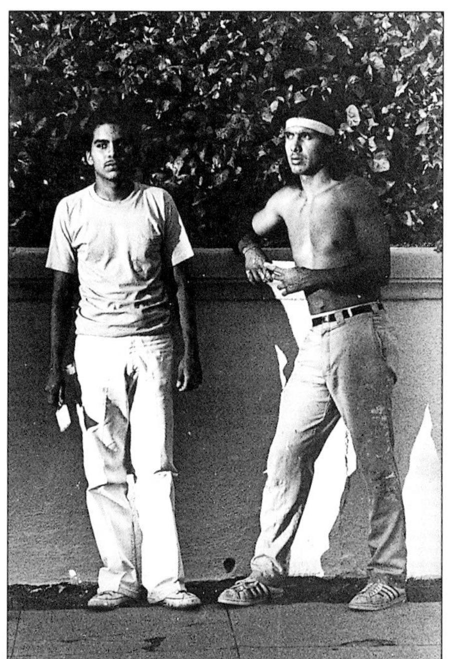

Peter Quezada (right) and Eddie Olivares, June 1980.

official demise of this program, he returned to banking for full-time employment. Quezada continues to paint his murals and address the problems of gang violence and graffiti in his spare time, and he has earned a certain amount of renown and respect. He has been varyingly referred to by newspaper reporters and by those who live near his murals as the "the graffiti warrior," "Painter Pete," and "the Pied Piper" (the last title referring to his effectiveness in working with and interesting area youth in his projects).

Quezada's project is feasible largely due to the public's perception of mural painting, which in turn was affected by the mural activity of the late 1960s. Often inherent in discussions about graffiti and murals is the relativization of the two forms, the primary distinction revolving around the issue of legitimacy or official sanction. Murals tend to be regarded as "artistic" and "constructive" and in general are a more socially accepted activity. Such a perception obscures the ambiguity of issues and motivations involved in painting on public walls. For example, an organization in Sylmar came under fire for its efforts to replace graffiti with murals painted by local tagging crews. Residents perceived the use of spraycans in the painting of the murals as an endorsement of graffiti. On the other hand, one of the largest gangs in Los Angeles has painted (with brushes, not spraycans) at least three murals explicitly announcing their name on the walls of private businesses who granted them permission. When Quezada recently attended a neighborhood police forum about gang problems, he watched a slide presentation that included several images of his work and heard his murals characterized in the context of gang promotion.

Today there are numerous mural painting projects operating around Los Angeles County and sponsored by either small neighborhood organizations or larger citywide programs. Quezada notes that each group has its own criteria regarding where and how to undertake a project, and that he simply works according to his own set of principles. For example, he avoids explicit reference to any particular gangs in his murals so as not to promote such affiliations. He includes a "roll call" in all of his murals, a term that also refers to an element used by gangs and graffiti crews whereby the individual names of the members of the group that is announcing itself are listed. Quezada's roll calls consist of the names of the people who assisted on the murals (plate 6). These names are usually painted against the motif of a scroll. While many of the kids Quezada works with are gang members or taggers, he will not use their gang names or nicknames in a roll call. The only times nicknames show up in his murals are when he does not know the people by any other name and when he is commemorating those who have died.

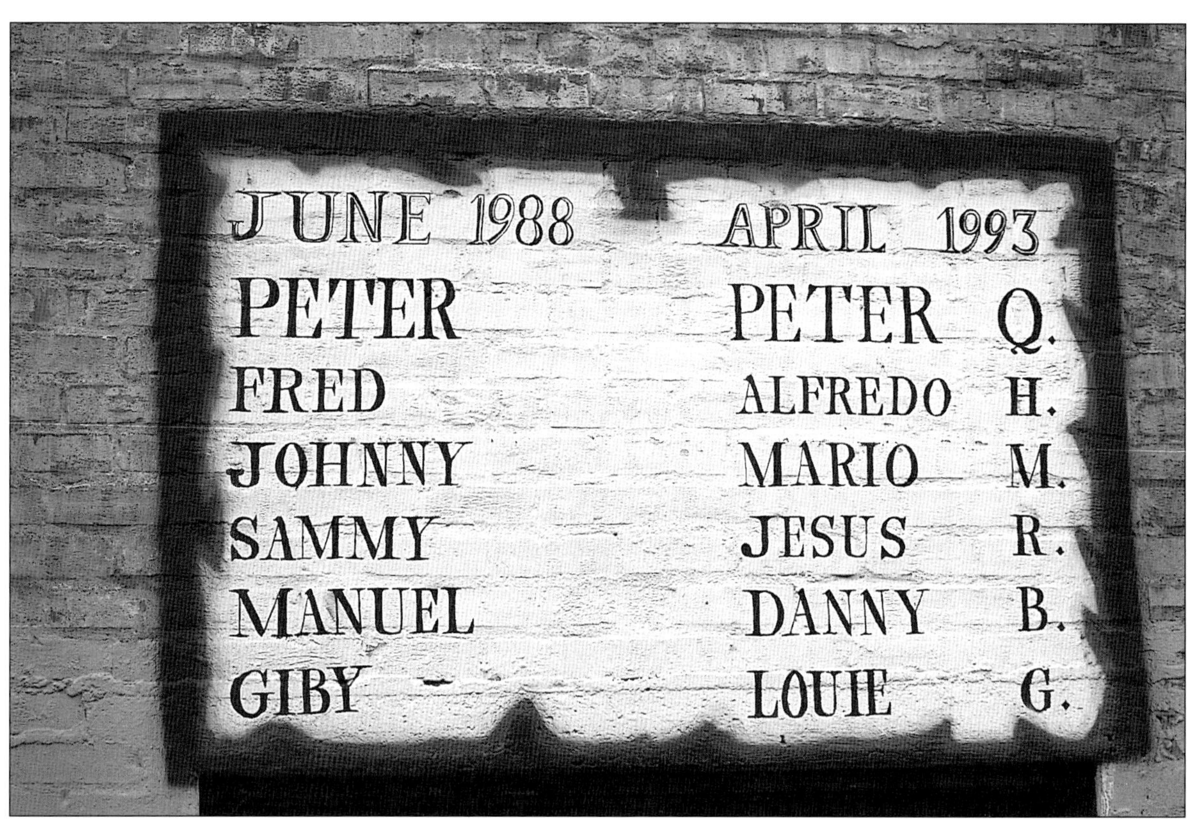

"Roll Call" or "honor roll" with Caslon lettering.

Quezada primarily works alone, with assistance coming from area youth he has met over the years or whom he meets while he is painting. Consequently he does not have to subscribe to the regulations or directives of a larger organization. Quezada's projects bypass most of the usual procedures necessary for getting a public art piece implemented and installed. He does not wait for approval for his designs or sites. While he does plan his text and the images he will use, the mural's entire composition emerges while he is painting and is dependent on the contours of the particular surface and the space available. Quezada has painted a modest amount of work on commission for businesses, and he has also received a contract from the city of Los Angeles for the painting of two retaining walls. For the most part, however, his work occurs without official approval, without external funding, and with an understanding that their pristine form is ephemeral. Quezada paints on public and privately owned property; the surfaces include garages, fences, retaining walls, and businesses. He is occasionally confronted by the owners of property on which he is painting as well as by gang members whose graffiti he is erasing, and he has been questioned by the police while working, but no one has ever taken legal action against him.

Quezada will touch up his murals from time to time if they fade or get tagged, but on the whole, he is fairly resigned to their vulnerability. He repeatedly acknowledges: "If you paint in public you've got to realize the probability of your piece being hit up—every time you do a mural, you are really just rolling the dice that it will be accepted by the people in the area."

In fact, Quezada's work has had remarkable longevity. His murals are a ubiquitous part of the concrete landscape along Figueroa Street, a major thoroughfare in Highland Park; few pieces exhibit much graffiti. In the spring of 1994, Quezada painted a piece on commission that has been subject to more vandalism than any of his other murals. The owner of an auto shop in his El Sereno neighborhood asked him to paint *la Virgen de Guadalupe* on the wall of his store. This wall had been hit up continually by graffiti writers. The image of Guadalupe was chosen because she is a popular and respected figure among many Mexican Catholics. A particularly Mexican manifestation of the Virgin Mary and the patron saint of Mexico, she is revered for her clement nature. Her image has also been evoked in revolutionary contexts both in Mexico and in the United States: by Father Hidalgo in the 1810 uprising against Spanish colonial rule of Mexico; by Zapatistas during the Mexican Revolution; and by the United Farm Workers under César Chávez. The image of *la Virgen de*

Guadalupe is also often used in gang and prison contexts in both tattoos and commemorative murals.

Quezada based the image in his Guadalupe mural on a framed picture that hangs inside the store. Alongside the figure of Guadalupe, he painted the following text: "*Si Tienes Penas O Problemas, Yo Te Los Resolvere.* If You Have Problems Or Miseries I Shall Resolve Them" (plate 11). Several days after the completion of the mural, black spray paint covered the entire figure of Guadalupe. Quezada repainted the image. A few days after this, a bucket of white paint was thrown onto the image of *la Virgen*. Because Quezada had applied a protective coat of graffiti-guard to the mural he was able to wash off this layer of paint. After this incident, a local priest blessed the mural, and flowers were set in front of it. A few days later, blue paint was thrown onto the image of *la Virgen*. The store owner, not realizing the paint was water soluble, tried to remove it with paint thinner, which stained the entire figure a dark blue. Quezada does not take this attack personally. He speculates that the culprit was making an antireligious statement. It is also possible that the vandalism of the mural was prompted by denominational antagonism; some Fundamentalist Christians regard Catholic reverence for the Virgin Mary as a threat to the primacy of Christ.

Quezada indicates that neither his name nor the names of his assistants, which he includes in all of his pieces, have ever been crossed out. Among graffiti writers such a practice is a gesture of confrontation and disrespect. The messages and marks inscribed on walls are taken very seriously by those who read and write them. Members of a local gang recently graffitied their moniker on a part of one of Quezada's murals. They also tagged the facade of an abandoned store adjacent to the mural. Shortly thereafter, members from a rival gang drove by and fired shots into this wall.

The Sites

The battles for preeminence among different gangs are manifest in the writings on the walls. The names that appear and cancel out one another reflect the centrality of the concept of place to such alliances: 18th Street, El Sereno, Highland Park, Avenues Cypress, Avenues 43rd, Diamond Street, Temple Street, DogTown. Revolving around the idea of "neighborhood," Los Angeles's earlier Chicano gangs expressed their pride and fellowship for the place and friends among which they had grown up. Quezada states:

The neighborhood concept is something that when you're growing up from a certain area, the friends that you hang around with, the people that you hang around with, and you yourself formulate this feeling of pride for where you grew

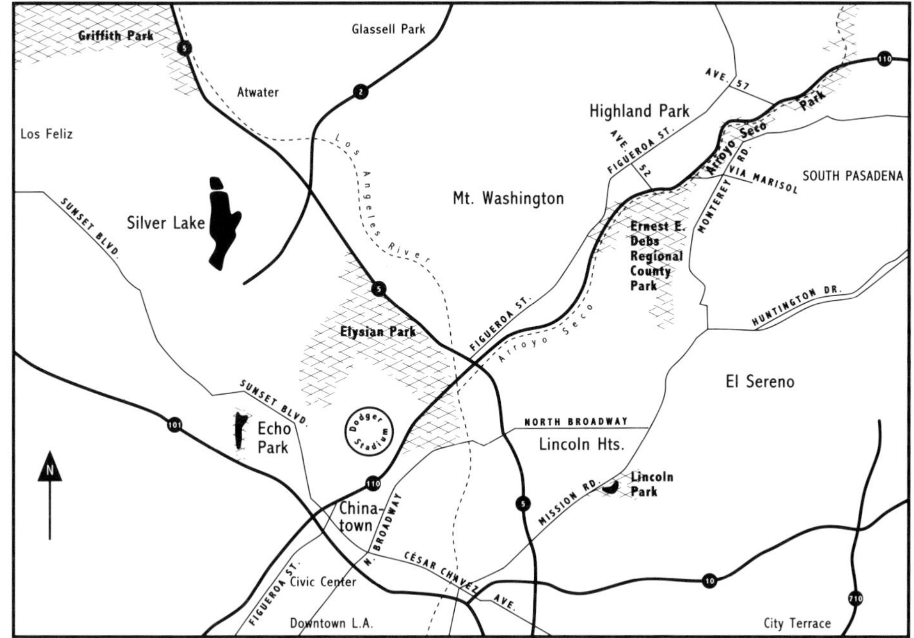

Map of northeast Los Angeles.

up and the friends you grew up with. So pretty soon you form what is known as a neighborhood.

When I was growing up, it was the same thing. I grew up in Echo Park. I took—whether you call it false pride or whatever you want to call it—I took pride in being from that area, to the point where that's how the gangs start. To my credit, I never once burglarized somebody's house, did drugs, or any of that negative stuff that's associated with gangs now. But at the same time, I was from something that was known as a neighborhood, and in this case I was from the Echo Park neighborhood. I could have been from the 18th Street gang, I could have been from the Diamond Street gang, I could have been from the Temple Street gang—any number of gangs that were around in those days I could have belonged to but I had no pride in them. I had no desire to be from them. I was from where I lived. I lived in the Echo Park area and I was from Echo Park.

It's very, very hard for somebody that didn't grow up in a neighborhood to relate to the things I'm saying. It's really hard to explain. It's a matter of feeling. You have to feel it. And in my case, I had a deep feeling, naturally, for where I was from, and it would have been the same

thing if I was from any other neighborhood.

Urban geography is mapped according to many different imperatives and perceptions. There is no central body that officially designates neighborhoods in Los Angeles. In 1985, the city planning department identified 53 "centers," and the department of transportation had manufactured some 433 signs designating neighborhood identity in response to citizen requests, while the much-relied-upon Thomas Brothers street map listed 70 "communities." The National Commission on Neighborhoods states: "In the last analysis, each neighborhood is what the inhabitants think it is" (Downs, 13). "Neighborhood," then, is subjectively defined, and local geographies as well are conceived in varying and specific terms that do not correspond with mapped geographies or municipal designations.

To appreciate the work of Peter Quezada, it is necessary to recognize his relationship to the physical and social topography of the areas where he paints. Quezada's murals are generated as much in response to the physical landscape of areas in which he has lived as to the intangible quality of his experiences there. His work is mainly visible in the neighborhoods of Echo Park, Silver Lake, Lincoln Heights, El Sereno, and Highland Park. Most of his recent work is in El Sereno, where he currently resides, but he is planning a piece for the neighborhood where he grew up, Echo Park.

The Los Angeles River runs between downtown Los Angeles and East L. A., which is probably the best known and largest Chicano community in the United States. The river has been a means by which some people conceive of the "eastside" and "westside" of the city—revealing the difference between how local or neighborhood geographies are drawn and understood by those who live there and those who do not. Silver Lake and Echo Park lie west of the river, while the other neighborhoods in which Quezada paints lie east of it. He states: "Originally, I'm a Westsider. A lot of people don't understand this; especially people who call Westwood and West L. A. the Westside. But when we were kids, we were considered Westsiders. When I was from Echo Park, I wasn't just from Echo Park, I was from Westside Echo Park."

Though divided by the river, the topography and demography of the neighborhoods where he paints are similar in some respects. In all of these neighborhoods there are substantial Spanish-speaking populations—both older and more recent communities of immigrants—with increasingly visible Southeast Asian immigrants. Some of Quezada's murals contain imagery familiar to Mexican vernacular expressions and history, and he sometimes

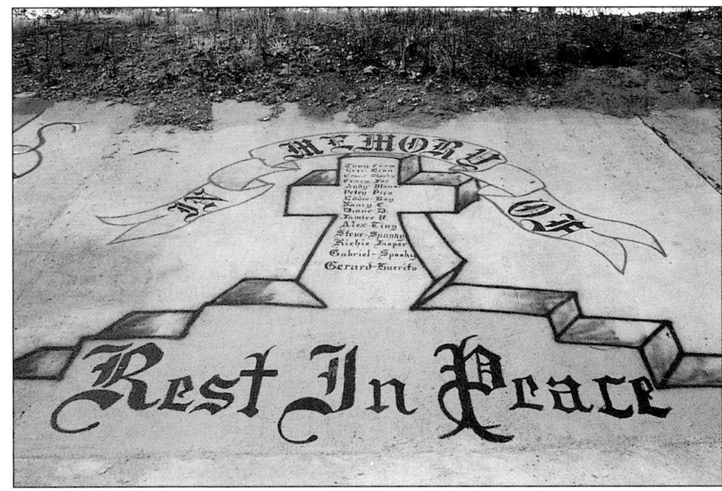

This cross memorializes people Peter has known who were associated with an area gang. The cross is one of a series of images to which Peter has added since 1987. The wall is approximately twenty feet high, and the images extend horizontally along the wall for about a hundred feet.

writes his text in Spanish as well as English. All of these areas are hilly, with some residential dwellings located on the slopes that incline from the main boulevards and commercial areas. Cement retaining walls are built at the bases of these slopes; some also contain a system of stairways that connect the sidewalk to streets or buildings located higher up a hill.

The walls determine the contour and orientation of Quezada's murals, and because many of them are painted along retaining walls, his work tends to be horizontal in format. He also does not work with scaffolding, thus limiting the height of his murals to what he can reach from a six-foot ladder. There is, however, one site at which Quezada has continually painted since the 1980s where the potential height of his pieces is substantially increased: the walls of the Arroyo Seco.

The Arroyo Seco is a tributary that feeds into the Los Angeles River from the northeast. For part of its distance it runs parallel to the 110 Pasadena Freeway, and segments of it are visible to passing traffic. After two severe floods in the 1930s, the U. S. Army Corps of Engineers began an extensive project of channelizing the river and its major tributaries. Miles of river were reduced to narrow trickles retained by heavy concrete walls on either side. These walls, which at some points extend up to forty feet, are not vertical but incline at approximately forty-five-degree angles from the ground so that it is possible to walk up and down them. Such a surface has enabled Quezada to paint pieces as tall as thirty-five feet.

It is on the walls along the Arroyo Seco that Quezada honed his skills as an artist. Here also, in his words, "many graffiti writers graduated from being graffiti writers to graffiti artists." Photographs that Quezada took of these walls in the mid-1980s reveal artwork using themes and images he would later incorporate in the murals painted on surface streets (plates 5, 7).

The walls of the Arroyo Seco on which Quezada has painted are those that run through his old neighborhood of Highland Park. Public parklands and recreation areas border the eastern side of this area. One must descend to get down to the riverbed. The walls and walkways on

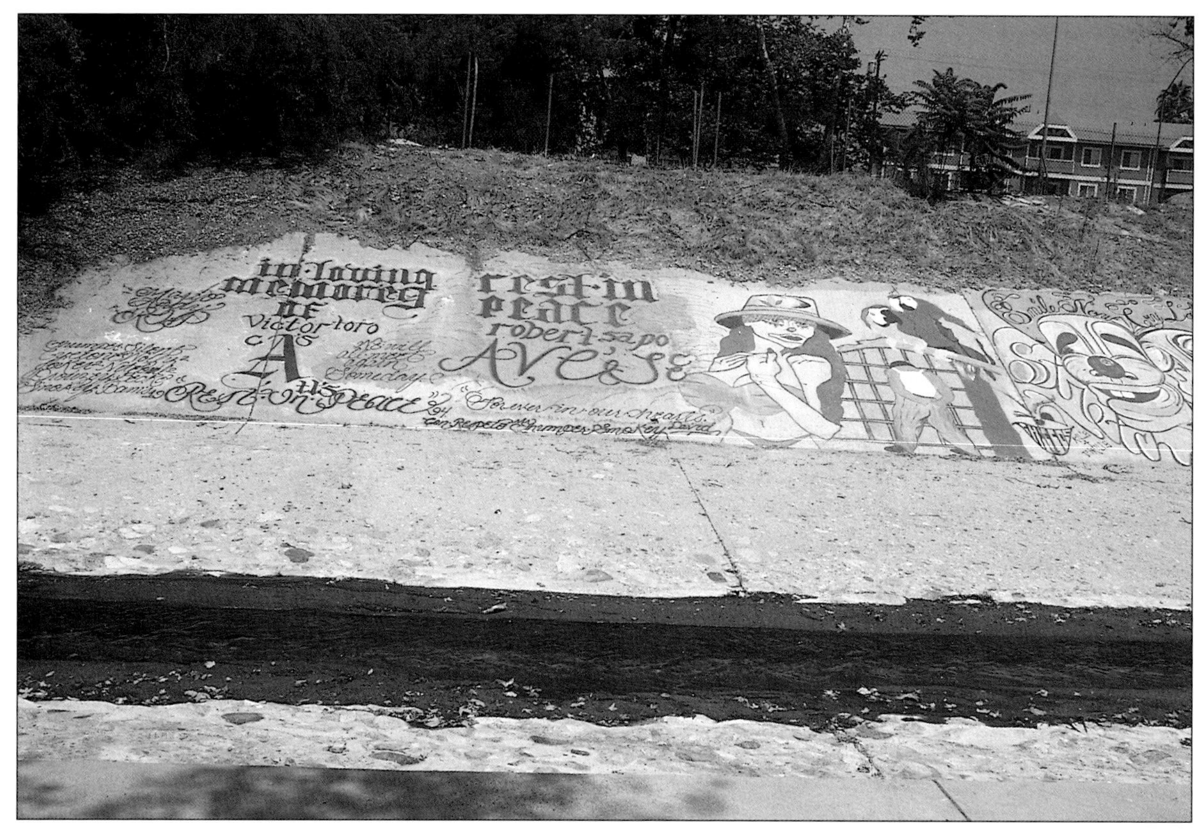

Part of the series painted along the Arroyo Seco by Peter and his friends Eddie, Rudy, and Stretch. The writing on the far left side commemorates a group of youth who died in a car accident. This message was painted by friends of the victims and appended to Peter's mural.

either side give more of the impression of a freeway or drainage spillway than the banks of a river. A series of pieces, some faded from the sun or painted over by newer works, lies off of the Via Marisol exit from the Pasadena Freeway. Some of these pieces share similar subject matter, while others seem to be more thematically incongruent. They include a lowrider that was painted by Quezada and his friend Stretch; a tribute to British ska music; *la Virgen de Guadalupe;* the head of Jesus Christ; a large cross memorializing members of the Avenues gang who have died; the masks of tragedy and comedy. More recently Quezada has added the figure of a shackled prisoner in front of a guard tower, a buxom female character wearing a clown's mask, and a pair of green-and-red parrots. He had planned the next section to be the head of a white dog and had started to grid out the project when a car accident killed several teenagers who were associated with the Avenues. Friends of the victims spray-painted a commemorative message in that space. In selecting this spot on the wall—there are miles of available wall on either side of Quezada's work-in-progress—the writers expressed their respect for his piece; appending their message to his mural seems to indicate that they deemed the association appropriate.

Quezada has also painted along the walls that lie between the Avenue 43 and Avenue 52 exits off the Pasadena Freeway.

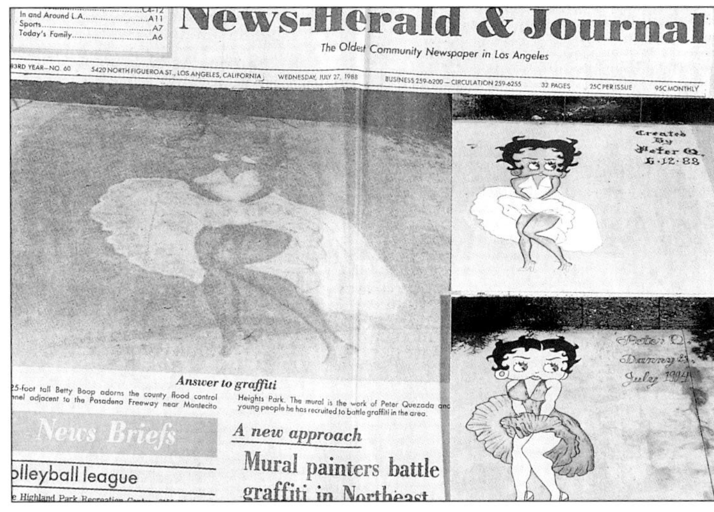

In and Around L.A. A11
Sports A7
Today's Family A6

News-Herald & Journal

The Oldest Community Newspaper in Los Angeles

3RD YEAR—NO. 60 5420 NORTH FIGUEROA ST., LOS ANGELES, CALIFORNIA WEDNESDAY, JULY 27, 1988 BUSINESS 259-6200 — CIRCULATION 259-6255 32 PAGES 25C PER ISSUE 95C MONTHLY

Answer to graffiti

25-foot tall Betty Boop adorns the county flood control nel adjacent to the Pasadena Freeway near Montecito Heights Park. The mural is the work of Peter Quezada and young people he has recruited to battle graffiti in the area.

News Briefs

olleyball league

A new approach

Mural painters battle graffiti in Northeast

The walls are especially high along this segment, rising up to about forty feet. In 1988, Quezada painted a twenty-five-foot Betty Boop character, which was subsequently painted over by the Army Corps of Engineers. In the summer of 1994, he returned to this spot and painted the same character thirty-five feet high with the assistance of his friend Danny. The walls in this area bear the tags of various individuals. Near the ramp there is one small figure of the Warner Bros. cartoon character Road Runner. Quezada indicates that these walls used to be filled with artwork because this stretch is visible to passing traffic on the Pasadena freeway. He and friends had put up large, colorful pieces, but all have since been whitewashed. He points to slivers of color along the bottom of the wall to indicate the work buried by the latest layer of paint.

The two photographs show the Betty Boop that Peter painted in 1988 (twenty-five feet tall) and the one he painted with his friend Danny in 1994 (thirty-five feet tall). Peter adhered the two photographs to an old newspaper that ran a picture of the 1988 Betty Boop. The two figures were painted in the same spot along the Arroyo Seco between Avenue 43 and Avenue 52.

Quezada's different murals essentially map the routes he takes or has taken in his daily life. All of the neighborhoods in which he paints are ones with which he has an affinity or to which he feels an obligation.

He will not paint on streets he does not use regularly: "I know most of the walls in the area because I live in El Sereno, and let's say if a wall's in Echo Park, I know those walls. Whatever wall that I've done, I know the wall. I've been living here in L.A. all my life so I know the walls that I'm doing and I already know the history behind them. And the history on them is that they are graffiti-covered and as soon as the graffiti comes off, they just get hit up again."

Quezada's work at CYGS brought him opportunities to paint murals in other neighborhoods. On the whole, he has found those efforts unsatisfying, due to the lack of an emotional connection to the areas. He now prefers to limit his work to El Sereno, where he has lived for the past few years. Many of the messages he writes on these walls express a desired sense of area pride and community. They range from the statements "Take Area Pride" or "Our Neighborhood Alley. Enjoy" to holiday greetings such as "Happy New Year 1994" or "Have a Safe and Happy Holiday Season." When Quezada talks about the centrality of the idea of neighborhood to his work, the sentiment for neighborhood has a different tone from that which he expressed about growing up in Echo Park: "The pride now that I have in the neigh-

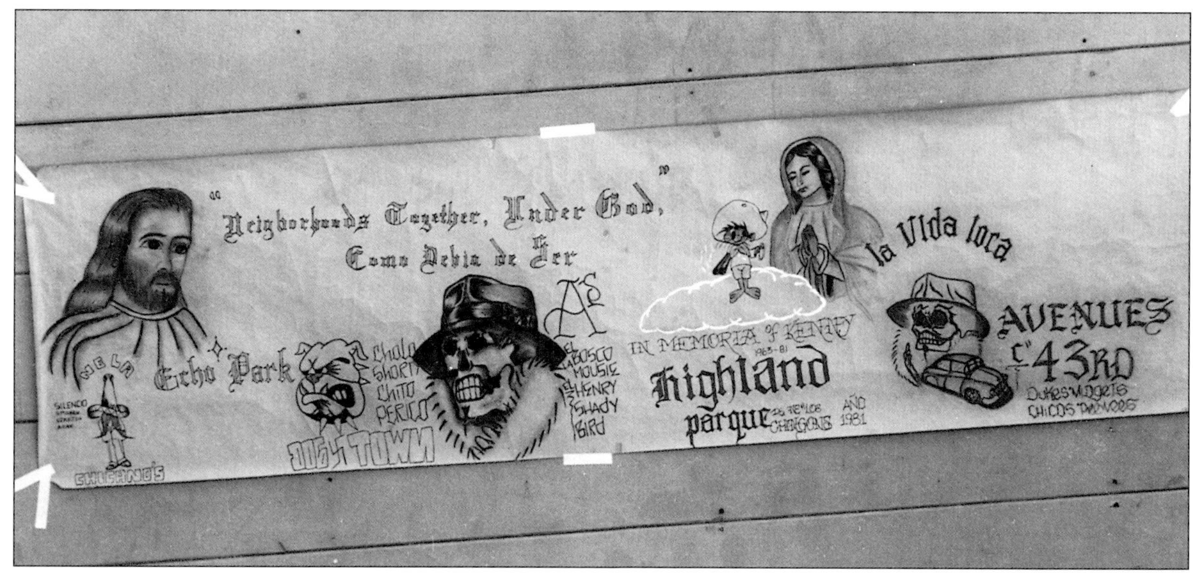

"Neighborhoods Together."

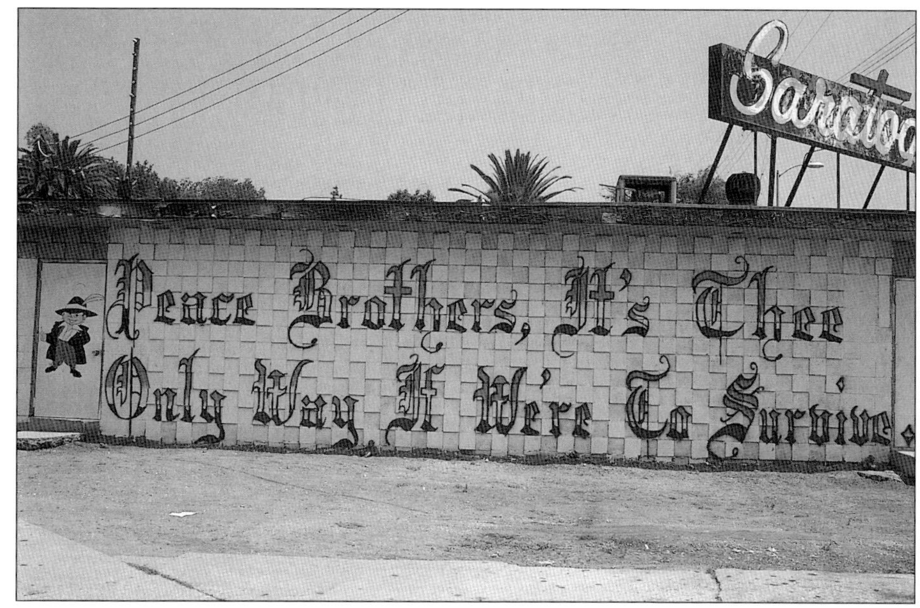

Mural painted in summer 1994 on an abandoned bar at Monterey Road and Huntington Drive in El Sereno.

borhood—the neighborhood that I live in, which is El Sereno, is a different thing. It's not for the gang that is known as El Sereno. I don't want to say I don't care about them because I have friends from El Sereno. But the thing is, I live in El Sereno community and I don't like seeing El Sereno community looking like a dump. So I do what I can to change that. Why should I go somewhere else when my little neighborhood looks like a dump?"

Before Quezada actually undertook the painting of murals to cover graffiti, he simply whitewashed walls. In the early 1980s, a Highland Park businessman whose building was repeatedly marked with graffiti wanted to make a statement regarding the need for businesses and residents to involve themselves in the maintenance of the area. He encouraged Quezada to have local gangs graffiti the wall of his business. Quezada invited the best artists from five different gangs to put up their names and symbols on the wall simultaneously: NELA (Northeast L.A.), Highland Park, DogTown, Avenues 43rd, Avenues Cypress. Quezada permitted members from Alpine Street to add their name, though they were not from the Highland Park area. Quezada also added the name of his old neighborhood, Echo Park.

Quezada and Philip Zamora, one of the people involved in the project, created a banner reproducing the images and writing from the wall. Included in the banner were drawings of Christ and *la Virgen de Guadalupe* looking down upon the gang symbols. The inscription Quezada added to the banner conveys the underlying point addressed in the project:

"Neighborhoods Together, Under God Como Debia De Ser [like it should be]"

July 2, 1994

After loading his truck with supplies, Peter sets out at noon to pick up two assistants who have been helping him paint over the graffiti on the walls of a bar in El Sereno that has been abandoned by its owners. Danny, eighteen years old, met Peter while playing handball in an area park. Alex, twelve years old, is a friend of Danny's.

The bar is located on a corner where the territories of three different gangs overlap. All four of the structure's external walls were covered with graffiti. The previous Saturday, Peter, Danny, and Alex had gone out to the site and begun painting. The walls are made of cinder block squares set so that they alternately project outwards in a checkerboard configuration. Because this surface is not flat and is too irregular for painting images, Peter decided to cover the walls with text and paint images on the three flat wooden doors. Last weekend, he and his assistants laid down a ground of beige over the graffiti on the front wall, and he spray-painted the

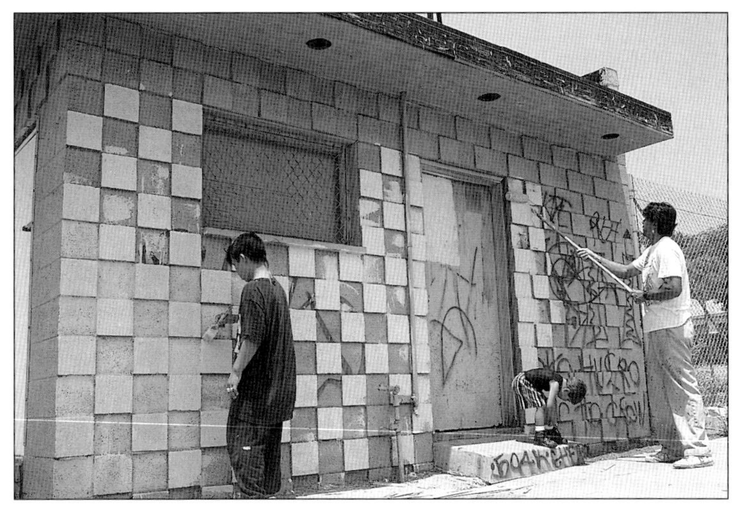

Peter, Peter-Bryan, and Alex painting over graffiti, July 1994.

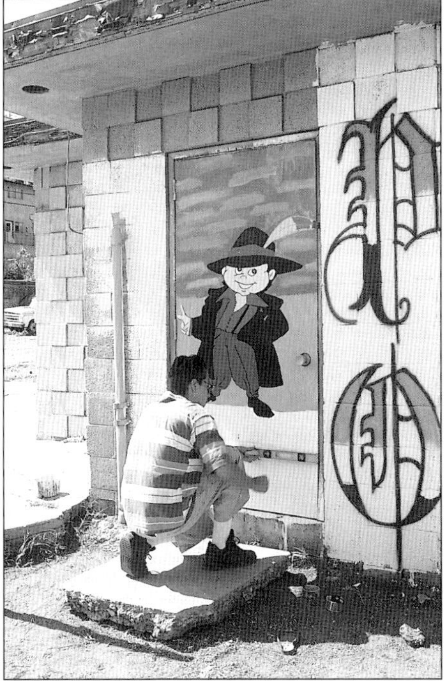

Danny uses a level to extend the frame of the *pachuco* character.

words: "Peace Brothers, It's Thee Only Way if We Are to Survive." Peter also drew in chalk a *pachuco* figure and a pair of parrots on the two doors that stand at either side of the text.

This weekend when they return to the site, they notice that three pink plaster angel figurines have been set in front of the wall that they are painting. (The angels are the work of Jill D'Agencia, a conceptual artist who has been setting these figures around the city in a gesture of protection.) Peter lays a tarp on the ground against the wall for his three-year-old son Peter-Bryan and leaves him to play there with his Power Ranger toys. Paints and mixing receptacles are unpacked from the milk crates in which they are stored (plate 1). Different color spraycans are carried in a mesh bag. Paintbrushes are selected from large water-filled plastic buckets that keep them from drying up when they are not being used. Paint is mixed and portioned into cardboard trays, the bottoms of milk cartons, or old tins. A small portable radio set on the ground is tuned to KRLA, "All Oldies Radio."

I arrive at the site as Alex and Peter go to the side of the bar and, using rollers, begin to paint over the graffiti. Peter's son wanders around from the front of the building and is given a small, hard-bristled brush to paint with. Danny works on the front wall, painting in the figure of the *pachuco*. Though he is facile with a spraycan, this is only his second time dealing with a paintbrush, and he is working carefully and slowly. The *pachuco* character he is rendering refers to the Mexican American youth of the 1940s who dressed in the zoot suit styles of the period. The zoot suit consisted of a long jacket and a pair of high-waisted, baggy trousers that were pegged at the ankle. This outfit was often embellished with a watch chain and wide-brimmed hat. In 1942, a group of young Mexican American men identified as "Zoot Suit Hoodlums" were charged with murder and criminal conspiracy at a trial in which their ethnic background was used by

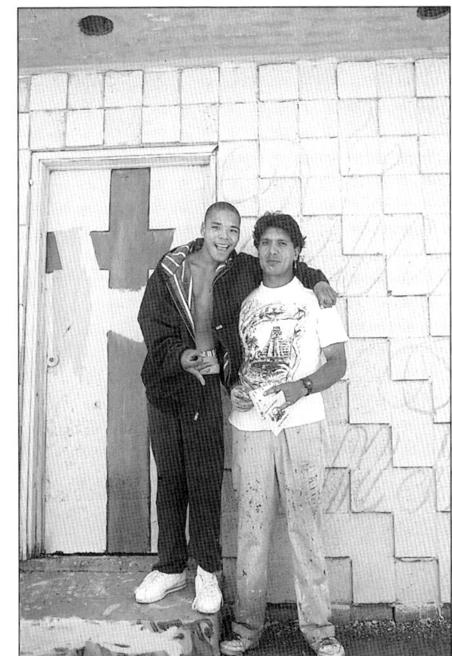

Peter and LaMark.

the prosecution as proof of guilt. Though nine of the men were convicted of murder, the court of appeals would later reverse the decision and concede that there had been a lack of evidence. In 1943, in what became popularly known as the "Zoot Suit Riots," bands of U.S. servicemen attacked Mexican American men in East Los Angeles, targeting in particular those who were wearing zoot suits. These circumstances contributed to the popular consideration of *pachucos* or zoot-suiters as persecuted rebels—forerunners to the Chicano civil rights movement—as well as the stylistic models for contemporary urban youth culture. Noting that he hopes to get fitted for a zoot suit himself in the near future, Danny says he is fond of the rendition of the *pachuco* he is painting because it is smiling, but at the same time the motives and emotions concealed by the smile remain hidden.

After Peter and his assistants have been painting about an hour, a white truck with the words *"Mariscos"* painted in blue on the side pulls up onto the sidewalk in front of the bar. The side of the truck opens out into a food counter, and plastic chairs are set outside for customers. Area residents wander by. Many stop and talk to Peter about the mural, wondering who had granted permission to paint but indicating approval and encouragement for the endeavor. At one point in the afternoon, Peter's wife, Michelle, drops by to bring soda, which is kept cool with ice provided by the food truck proprietors.

Peter uses a paintbrush to outline the letters of the text on the side of the bar. On either side of a door he outlines in cursive the words: "*Gozar la Vida* [Enjoy Life]" and "*Vivir en Paz* [Live in Peace]" (plate 8). Instead of working on the parrots that are already sketched in chalk on one of the front doors, he searches for an image to put on the door of the side wall. He goes to his truck and sorts through a stack of images stashed in the glove compartment. He selects a bookmark that is illustrated with a reproduction of Michaelangelo's *Piéta* and a cross draped with a swath of fabric. The latter is an image that he has painted before in an earlier mural (plate 9).

Alex, Peter-Bryan, and I are sent around to the other side of the bar to paint. After about a half hour, Alex and Peter-Bryan begin to antagonize each other and Alex uses his roller to paint Peter-Bryan's arms beige. Danny is absorbed in the details of the *pachuco* character. Peter is painting the background for the cross image. A young man approaches the building calling "Painter Pete! Painter Pete! Where's Painter Pete?" We direct him to the other side of the building. Peter asks me to take a picture of him and his friend LaMark. After I've taken one shot, LaMark turns and slides his shirt off so I can take a picture of the tattoo of his gang on his back. LaMark asks Peter if he will come up to the Rose Hills housing projects to produce a mural with some of the people who live up there. Peter offers to paint a rose on the other side of this building—which points in the direction of Rose Hills—and put up a memorial scroll commemorating the people from the area who have died.

It is beginning to get late by the time Alex and Peter-Bryan have colored in the letters on the side wall. Peter had wanted to outline the letters with a brush, but because of time limitations he decides to spray-paint the outlines. He prefers to outline with a brush because it leaves a crisper line and cleaner letter, whereas the overspray from a spraycan leaves a fuzzy line. When Peter has finished the letters, he walks around to the front of the building to survey Danny's painstaking work on the *pachuco* figure. He takes a brush and adds some birds in the background and shading to the clothing. "Damn," Danny says, "you make me look like an amateur."

The day's work ends with their packing up the painting supplies and swinging by the Arroyo Seco in order to plan the grid for a Betty Boop mural. Peter generally dedicates Saturdays to work on his mural projects, reserving Sundays for time with his family. It is a three-day weekend because Independence Day falls on a Monday this year, and so Peter returns to the abandoned bar by himself a day later to work on the parrots (plate 10). When he works alone and does not have to direct or supervise anyone else, he is able to focus his artistic attention more. Throwing in every color he has, he creates a vibrant and detailed image with which he is particularly pleased. Peter puts an emphasis on the use of interesting color combinations and the inclusion of details such as buttons on a coat or shading on a figure. It is such inclusions that, in his words, "add color" or "flavor" to the murals and as such reduce the likelihood of their defacement. The following week, after he and Danny complete the Betty Boop mural at the river, they return to the abandoned bar and paint the scroll and roll call next to the parrots.

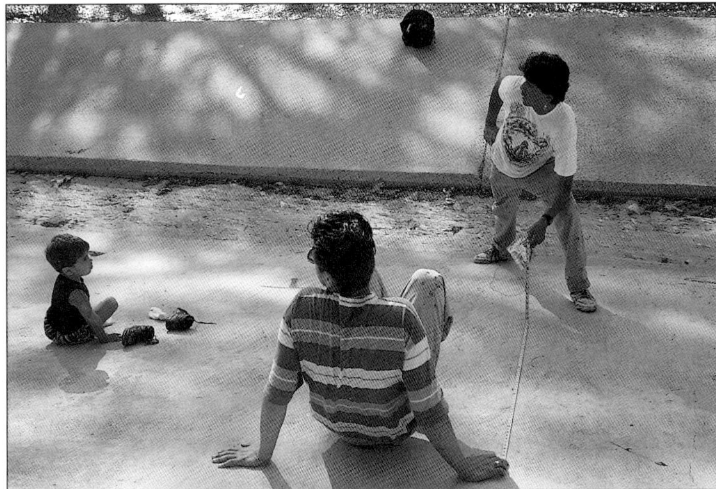

Peter and Danny calculate the dimensions of the grid for the Betty Boop mural. Peter's son, Peter-Bryan, looks on.

The Pieces

The Grid

Quezada insists that his artistic efforts are the result of much deliberate hard work and practice. His first endeavors were produced with a spraycan under the guidance of a thirteen-year-old graffiti writer. Quezada followed him around, observing how he held the can, how close he held the can to the wall he was writing on, and how he moved his hand and arm to create smooth lines. Little by little, Quezada informally picked up skills and methods from other friends and acquaintances. When recalling his early works, he laughs and dismisses them as "the work of a kid—in terms of art," and he sometimes refers to himself as "King of the B-murals." It is perhaps because Quezada did not have a natural inclination toward art and instead had to develop his artistic skills conscientiously—"learning the hard way through repetition and practice"—that he is so adamant about the use of "the grid" in the execution of his work.

"The grid" refers to a technique commonly used by artists or anyone else who must translate images to different scales. Muralists almost always sketch their designs using a grid: the original artwork or design for the mural is divided into squares so that a grid covers the entire image. The dimensions of the mural are calculated, and a large grid proportionate to the smaller one is marked on the wall with chalk. In this way the proportions of the original small artwork are transferred accurately to a larger scale on the wall through the comparing of relative parts within the squares of the grid.

Quezada's use of this method developed out of a chance discovery while he was painting the twenty-five-foot Betty Boop on the wall of the Arroyo Seco in 1988. He had been trying to copy the image of Betty Boop from a postcard, but each time he stood back to assess his progress, he was puzzled by the disproportion between the legs and the head. Using a stick he found in the wash, he measured on the postcard how many head lengths could fit into the length of the leg. Using a larger stick, he measured the head of the figure on his mural and then measured the

"If you want to dance, you've gotta pay the fiddler." This text refers to the popular gangster saying "If you want to play, you've got to pay." This is part of a mural Peter was commissioned to paint on the exterior walls of a court stenographer's office in Highland Park on Figueroa Street near Loreto Street.

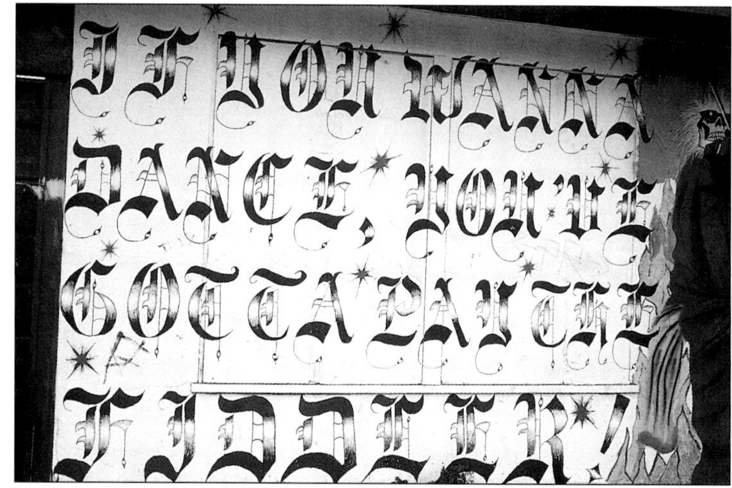

corresponding amount for the legs. He states: "So with that stick, just a stick, there were no exact measurements, no inches, no feet, it was all guestimation. I made it longer—I made the body longer. But making it longer, I had to make it wider. So that was my first measuring device. And that was my first grid."

A few months later, Quezada transferred the character of the Joker from a comic book to a wall by using a simple four-square grid (the image was divided in half vertically and horizontally). Quezada insists that a mural is only as good as the grid. It is, he states, evoking the metaphor of battle, his "best weapon." He begins every mural project by preparing the grids for each of the images he plans to paint. He adheres the original artwork to cardboard and then covers them with cellophane wrapping. The grid is applied to the cellophane with a pen; horizontal lines are labeled by number, vertical ones by letters of the alphabet.

When Quezada began to paint, he chose images that were part of the visual repertoire of gang youth. This included lettering styles, cartoon characters, cars, and religious iconography. Lyrics from popular songs, gang sayings, didactic messages, and general community messages make up the text that is a central component of Quezada's murals. Some of his work explicitly admonishes against certain types of behavior and activities: "Drinking and Drugs Aren't Magic; Don't Do 'Em"; "Pray to End Gang Violence" (plate 12); "Have the Courage to Say No to Gangs." He acknowledges that many of his messages are corny, but he emphasizes that these phrases occupy space on the wall that would otherwise be subject to graffiti. More important, he indicates that what his murals say does not matter as much as how they they are written, for the youth he is targeting read the letters as much as the words.

Lettering

Quezada identifies the three lettering styles he most uses as Old English, Script, and Caslon, all of which have been adopted by gang members and/or inmates. Old English is the most common form, appearing in graffiti and in T-shirt and other graphics, as well as being used for tattoo inscriptions. Script/cursive generally is used more frequently in tattooing than in graffiti. Caslon is the name for an old-style roman typeface that is used in gang graffiti, to a lesser extent than Old English.

The connotative—versus denotative—function of letters is often overlooked. Those who display the written word in public—whether as sign fabricators, graphic designers, or graffiti writers—are attuned to the formal quality of letterforms. That is, *how* something is said is as important as *what* is said. Quezada primarily uses Old English letters because they are "so classic." The use of Old English among Chicano youth in Southern California dates back to as early as the 1940s when individuals in car clubs and gangs, noting the use of Old English on "official" documents such as draft notices and diplomas, appropriated the letterforms for the inscription of their names, thus announcing themselves in a style that connoted authority and importance. In the 1970s, Jerry and Sally Romotsky identified three recognizable and consistent alphabet styles among graffiti writers, and they suggested that the most prevalent one, Point, was derived from Old English. The Romotskys indicate that Old English tended to be reserved for larger inscriptions to communicate "dignity and prestige" (Romotsky, 21) but was not used often due to the complexity of its form.

Old English lettering is also known as Black Letter or Gothic, and it was derived from the calligraphy of scribes during the medieval period. It has been suggested by scholars of typography that one factor contributing to the particular form of the letters was the scarcity of manuscript parchment: the condensed angularity of the letters allowed more text to fit on a page. Another factor was that the writing implement of this period was a flat-ended tool that naturally produced the variations in stroke width that are characteristic of Old English letters. The high value placed on the fine execution of letterforms reverberates in the contemporary use of the term "style," which was derived from the word "stylus," the writing implement of the medieval period. The term "style" is now used to qualify ways of executing a broad range of behaviors and artistic endeavors.

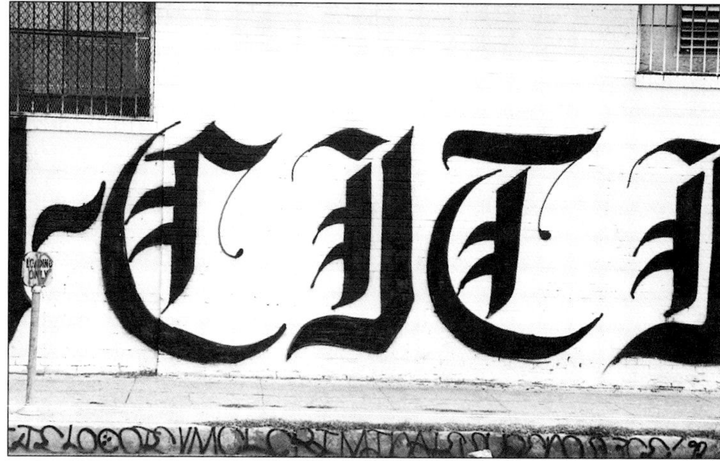
Old English graffiti in Mid-City area.

When Jerry and Sally Romotsky used the term "barrio calligraphy" to discuss graffiti, they were aptly emphasizing the importance of style and form in graffiti. Control and fluidity must be brought to the laying down of different lettering styles if they are to be consistent in form. While individual style is central to lettering in some types of graffiti, when conventional letterforms such as Old English are employed in graffiti, style is enunciated through convincing replication rather than idiosyncratic flair.

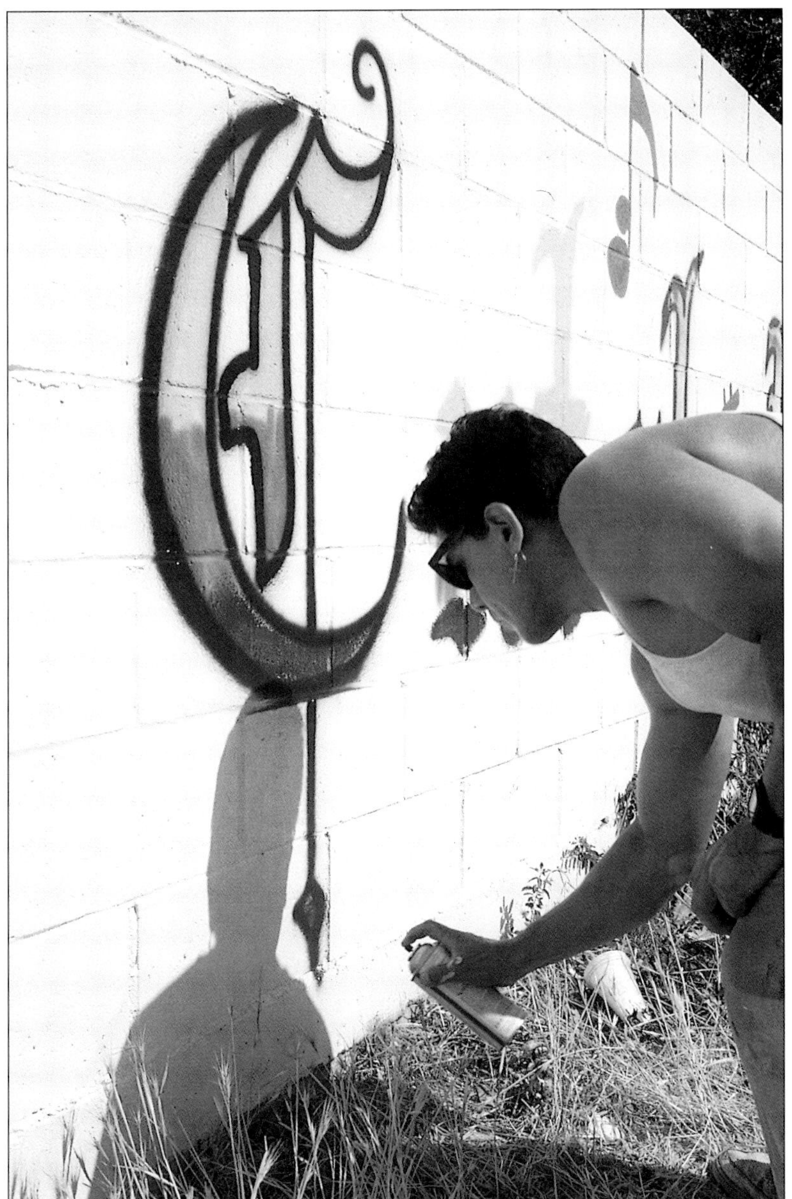

Multi-colored, Old English letters painted with a brush and spraycan. The phrase on the wall is taken from an old Rhythm & Blues song: "Later Baby, catch you on the rebound."

The examples of Old English visible on walls in Los Angeles today attest to the practice that is necessary for someone to perfect the forms and then paint them evenly on a large scale, illegally and with a medium that does not naturally lend itself to these forms. As the Romotskys found in the 1970s, most gang graffiti is not written in Old English. The letters most often used by gangs are sometimes generically referred to as "blocks"—when the Romotskys were writing, "Block" referred to a specific style that has since developed variations. These types of letters are less complicated, lacking the line variation, curves and angles of Old English. Quezada indicates that most gang members cannot write Old English but will have at least one associate who has taken the time to practice and learn the form.

Quezada initially practiced shaping and writing Old English and Script by working with pen and paper. By observing the technique of friends who were graffiti writers, he learned how to hold and move the spraycan to achieve the best lines. Quezada paints the letters in his murals with both a spraycan and a brush (plate 2). Sometimes he paints freehand with a spraycan, much the way a graffiti writer might. Other times he writes the letters on the wall in chalk or with a small paintbrush first.

Quezada models some of his lettering on the examples displayed in calligraphy books. He keeps photocopied pages of different lettering styles with his painting supplies, and he refers to them from time to time when he is painting. He indicates that finding these models can be difficult because aspiring graffiti writers often remove the Old English pages from calligraphy books in public libraries. Other sources for Quezada's letters are examples that are prevalent in daily urban living. These include printed forms, such as those found on packaging, signage, graffiti, and tattoos. Quezada has also cut out phrases of words from commencement programs, advertisements, and newspaper mastheads.

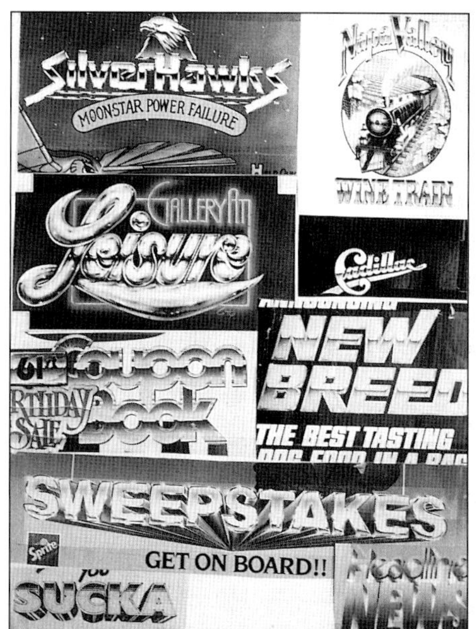

Letter style sheet.

He has created lettering style reference sheets for himself by taping various examples of a certain type of lettering onto a single sheet of paper.

Once Quezada became comfortable with these lettering styles, he adapted and changed them. He distinguishes between the Old English letters he paints in his murals and "hard-core gang letters." He softens the corners and points in his letters and usually paints them in multiple colors. When his letters are painted all black, he often paints them so that it looks as if light is reflecting off them, as if they were raised chrome letters. On the walls, these changes make his letters seem less severe than the lettering in gang monikers.

Images

As mentioned earlier, Quezada was not involved in the mural production of *el movimiento*. Nevertheless, many of the images and themes he paints were consolidated and displayed as aspects of a particularly Chicano cultural reservoir by the socially conscious artists working in the late 1960s and early 1970s. Among these staple figures and images are certain models of vintage cars; Mexican revolutionary figures; Aztec imagery (Indian princesses, warriors, pyramids); Catholic imagery and figures (crosses, *la Virgen de Guadalupe,* Jesus Christ); and the *pachuco*.

Images such as these continue to circulate in various mass-produced forms today. T-shirt graphics and theme magazines help embed these motifs as a cultural set in the public's mind, as well as generate an association between these iconic images and the representational figurative renderings, often found in prison or gang art, of prison scenery and life, scantily clad female figures, and *cholos* and *cholas* (dressed in baggy khakis and Pendletons or T-shirts).

Quezada draws many of the models for his gang-related themes from *Lowrider* and *Teen Angels* magazines. In fact, the flourishes that Quezada adds to his letters resemble the logotypes of these publications: *Teen Angels* in multi-color and *Lowrider* (though not in Old English) with chrome-like flashes and reflections. Both of these publications feature on their pages the artwork of predominantly Chicano urban readers. *Lowrider* is dedicated to the promotion of lowriding as a positive, creative expression. The regular issues con-

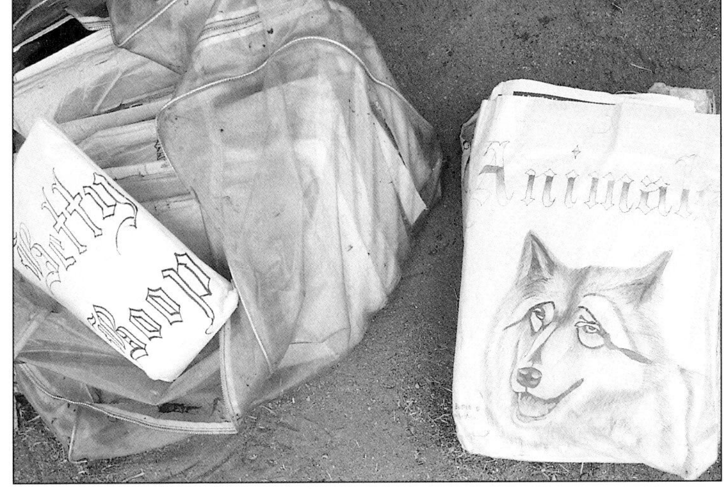

Envelopes in which Peter keeps his source imagery.

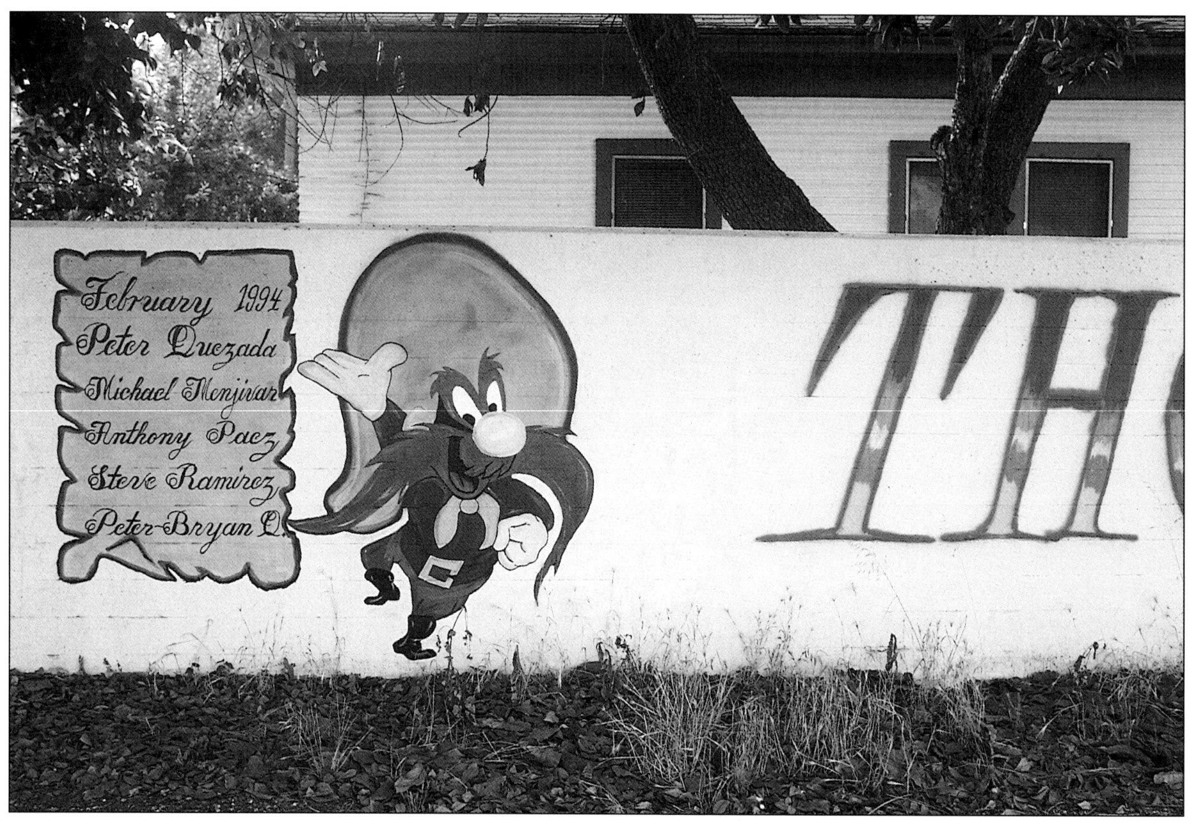

Warner Bros. character, Yosemite Sam, next to honor roll painted on a retaining wall along Huntington Drive in El Sereno. The phrase on the wall reads: "Though Shakin', Bakin', and Quakin' L.A.'s still #1."

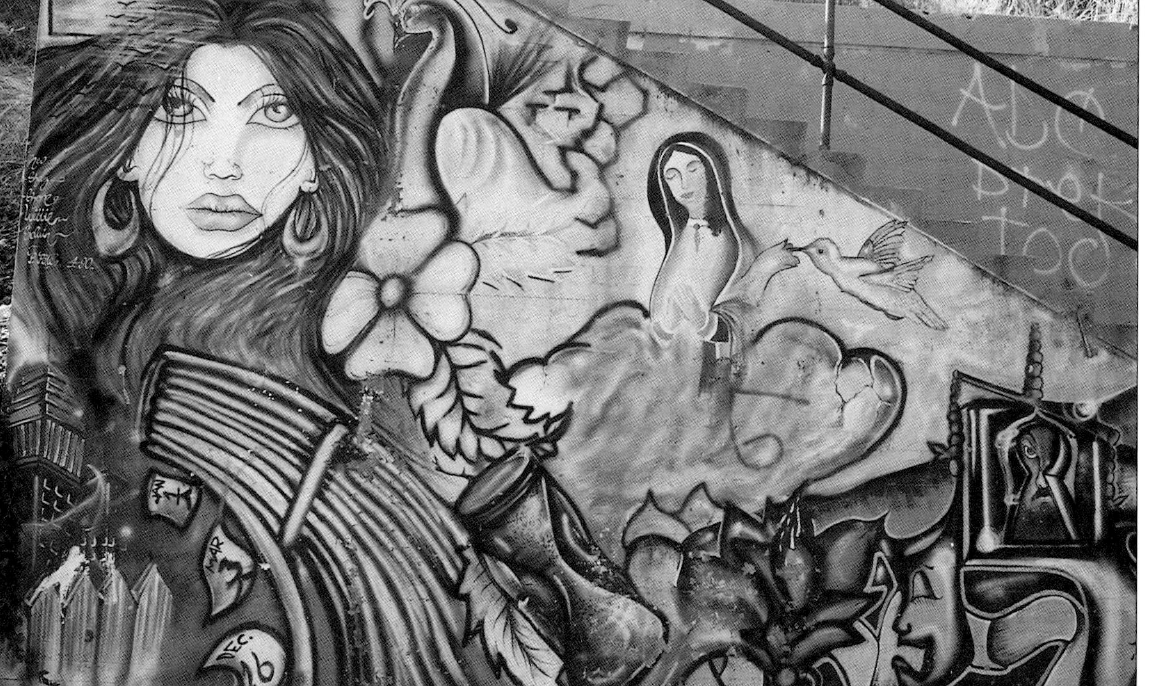

Composition and images were based on artwork printed in *Teen Angels.* Painted by Peter, Edwin, Willie, Robert, Frank, and Noel. Part of a series of images painted on Figueroa Street near Loreto Street in Highland Park.

tain letters from readers, articles, photographs of cars, and schedules of upcoming events. The magazine also publishes a supplement, *Lowrider Arte,* of readers' artwork. While "lowriding" refers to cars that have been customized (interior and exterior) and fitted with hydraulic systems that can raise or lower the body of the car, the magazine displays images of car customization in general and contains visual references to the 1940s and 1950s, the period when lowriding as well as other expressions of urban Chicano culture first flourished. *Teen Angels* displays the art and messages of gang members or incarcerated individuals. The art on its pages largely consists of messages or dedications from readers to one another. Consequently it features many examples of lettering.

Other icons or themes associated with gangs that Quezada uses are from the mass-produced images that abound in everyday life. For instance, it is a convention to inscribe the text of dedications or commemorative writings within the motif of either a scroll or a billowing ribbon. Quezada sometimes copies the scrolls he uses for text in his murals from the dedications in *Teen Angels,* but the first scroll he ever copied was from an advertisement in a 1970s surfing magazine. He has collected additional examples of scrolls from the labels of Cuervo Gold tequila bottles and other graphics from advertisements. When he does not use a scroll as the backdrop for his roll calls or messages, he will paint them against the image of an old, worn-looking piece of paper that he models on the "Wanted" posters from the Old West. Other images associated with gangs that Quezada has scavenged from the graphics on billboards and various printed ephemera such as newspapers and flyers include the masks of tragedy and comedy (from the popular gangster saying, "Smile Now, Cry Later"), clowns, skulls, and certain cartoon characters (from both Disney and Warner Bros.).

Quezada has a series of worn but carefully maintained 9" x 12" manila envelopes. On each envelope he has used either a ballpoint or felt-tipped pen to write carefully in Old English a description of the contents: Animal Art, Guns and Cars, Teen Angel Art, Betty Boop, Religious and Natural Art, Comic Book Art, Style Lettering, Stickers, magazine clippings, comic book art, religious pamphlets, bookmarks, and photos that he himself has taken constitute the contents of these envelopes. Quezada continually adds to these envelopes as he discovers potential material for his murals. He buys old magazines in bulk and will go out with his camera to document images that he thinks he would like to paint, such as cars and movie posters. He has also shot a series of photos of Betty Boop merchandise (postcards and T-shirts) at a boutique that recently sponsored a Betty Boop Fair. Quezada

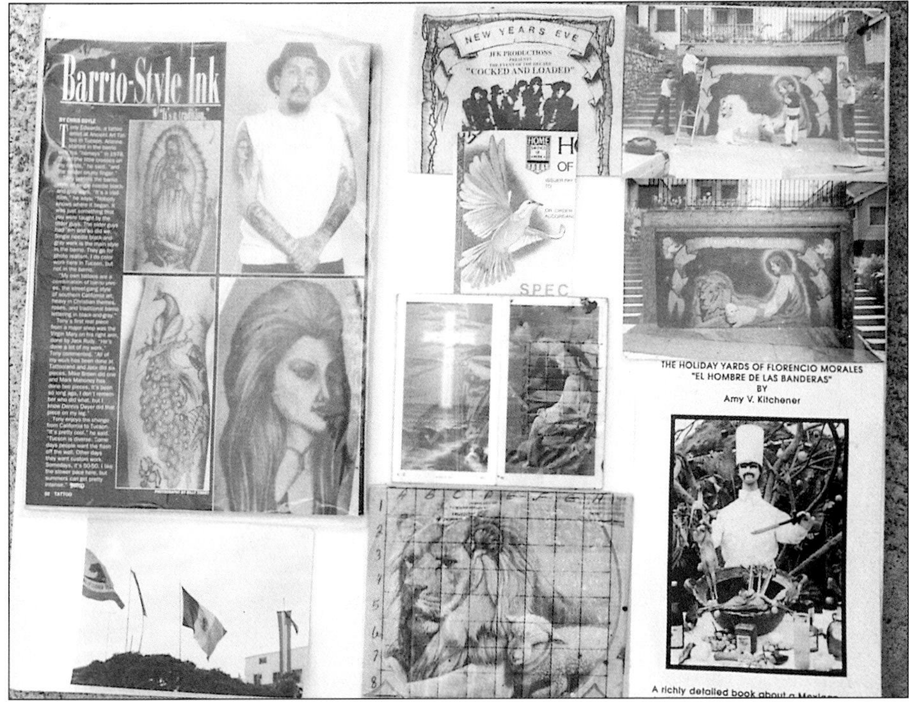

Peter compiled the sources for his commemorative mural of Florencio Morales and mounted them on a board for a presentation that was part of a program organized by Amy Kitchener in conjunction with the publication of her monograph on Florencio Morales (*The Holiday Yards of Florencio Morales: El Hombre de las Banderas.* University Press of Mississippi). The lion and lamb image was copied from a Jehovah's Witness pamphlet, the doves from American Express Traveler's Checks, the Christ from a prayer card, the peacock from a tattoo magazine (peacocks are popular gang images that symbolize long life), and the ribbon from the banner on an announcement for a local band.

states: "I bought some posters from a shop in Hollywood that was going out of business for fifty cents. So you see, I buy murals for fifty cents, a quarter. I see a picture on packaging from toys I buy for my kids, from advertisements, and I think 'There's a mural in this.' Everything that I paint, anyone could find or buy."

It is through Quezada's extraction of an image from its original context and its storage in his envelopes that a translation from mass media image to personal artistic resource occurs. Thus a lion from a Jehovah's Witness pamphlet retrieved from a garbage can is transformed into the central figure in a mural commemorating a neighbor of Quezada's who brought spirit and a sense of community to the area by decorating his yards for different holidays; the eagle on the cover of the U.S. Postal Service Express Mail envelopes finds its way into a tribute to American armed forces; and the skeleton from a Grateful Dead album is incorporated into a mural cautioning against gang involvement.

Many of the images that Quezada paints are drawn from his own personal interests and aesthetic considerations. The

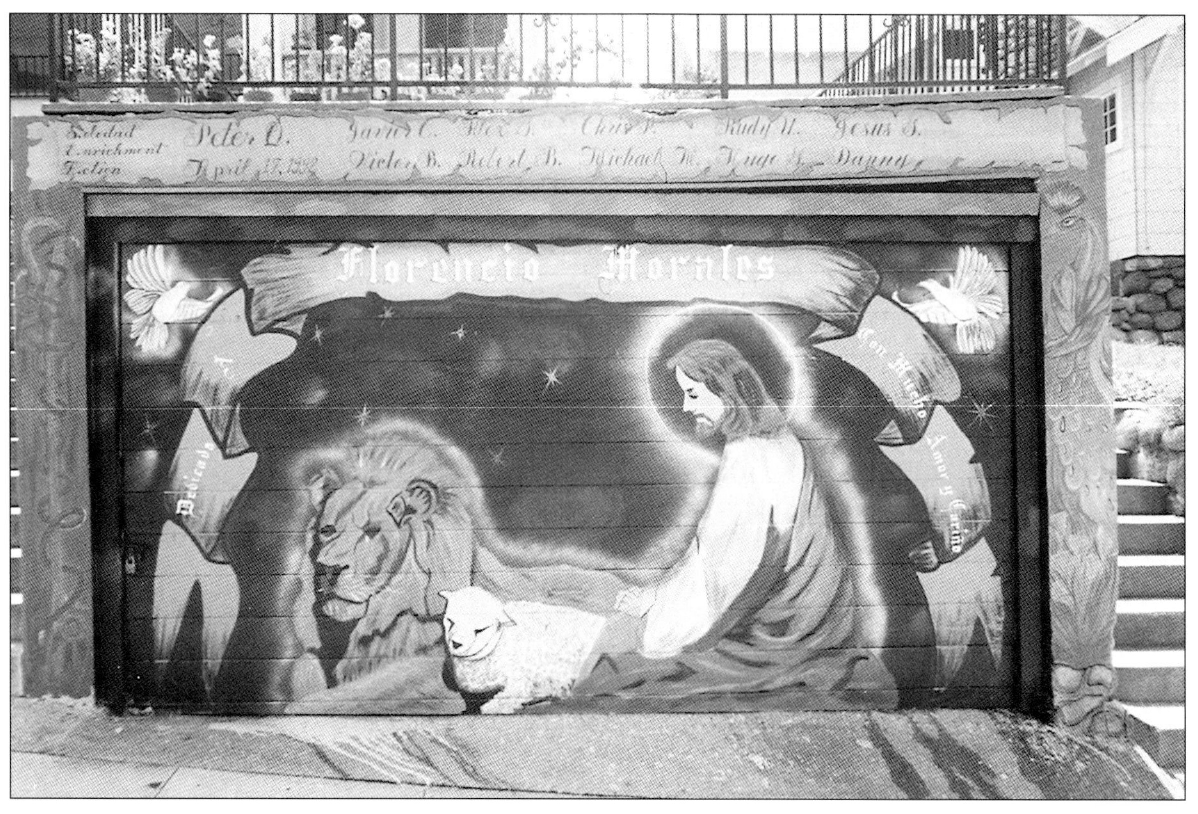

Mural commemorating Florencio Morales painted on Avenue 43 near Griffin Avenue.

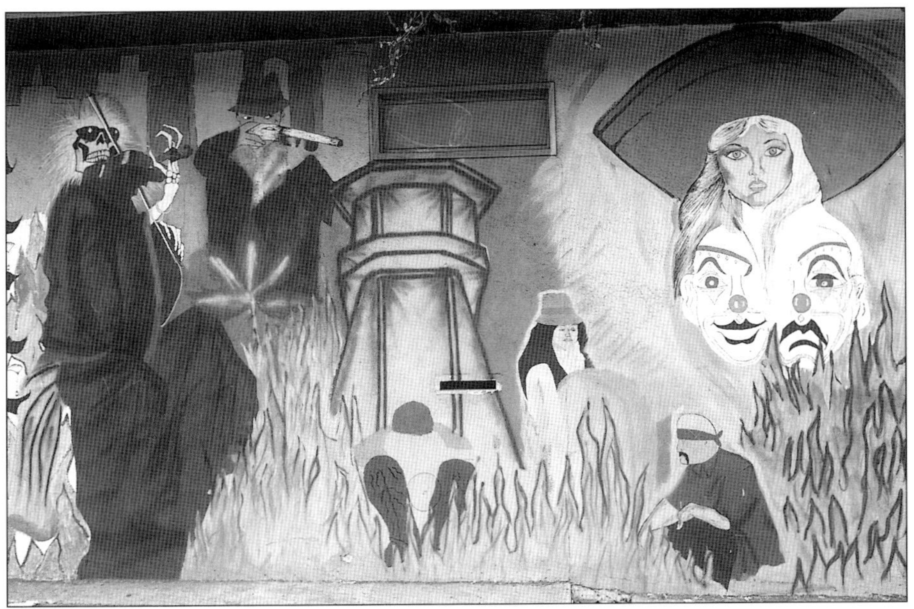

Segment of 9' x 32' mural painted on commission in Highland Park. The skeleton figure was copied from a Grateful Dead album cover.

walls and staircases near Nightingale Junior High School in Highland Park are covered with lettering and images that Quezada and a team of youth painted in 1990. The lower wall reads in Old English: "And the Lion Shall Lay Down with the Lamb Oh Lord, A Little Bit of Art Never Hurt Anybody, But a Little Bit of Graffiti Hurts a Lot of Bodies." Inside one stairwell is the message, in Old English: "Stop Gang Violence." Along the higher wall that runs up the hill are the words: "There will be peace in the valley." The text used was not so much a religious message as a quotation from a popular gospel song that has been recorded by several artists, including Elvis Presley, of whom Quezada is a big admirer.

Quezada's animal themes often perplex those who see his murals. He at one time had considered becoming a veterinarian, and his concern for and interest in animals carries over into his murals, sometimes creating unexpected juxtapositions. For instance, he painted a colorful duo of parrots just above the image of a shackled prisoner along the wall of the Arroyo Seco and (as described previously) next to the message "Peace Brothers, It's Thee Only Way if We're to Survive." Additionally, Quezada often paints himself and his three-year-old son as animals in his murals. In one, the father-son relationship is represented by a large polar bear hugging a little bear (plate 13). In another, a larger pen-

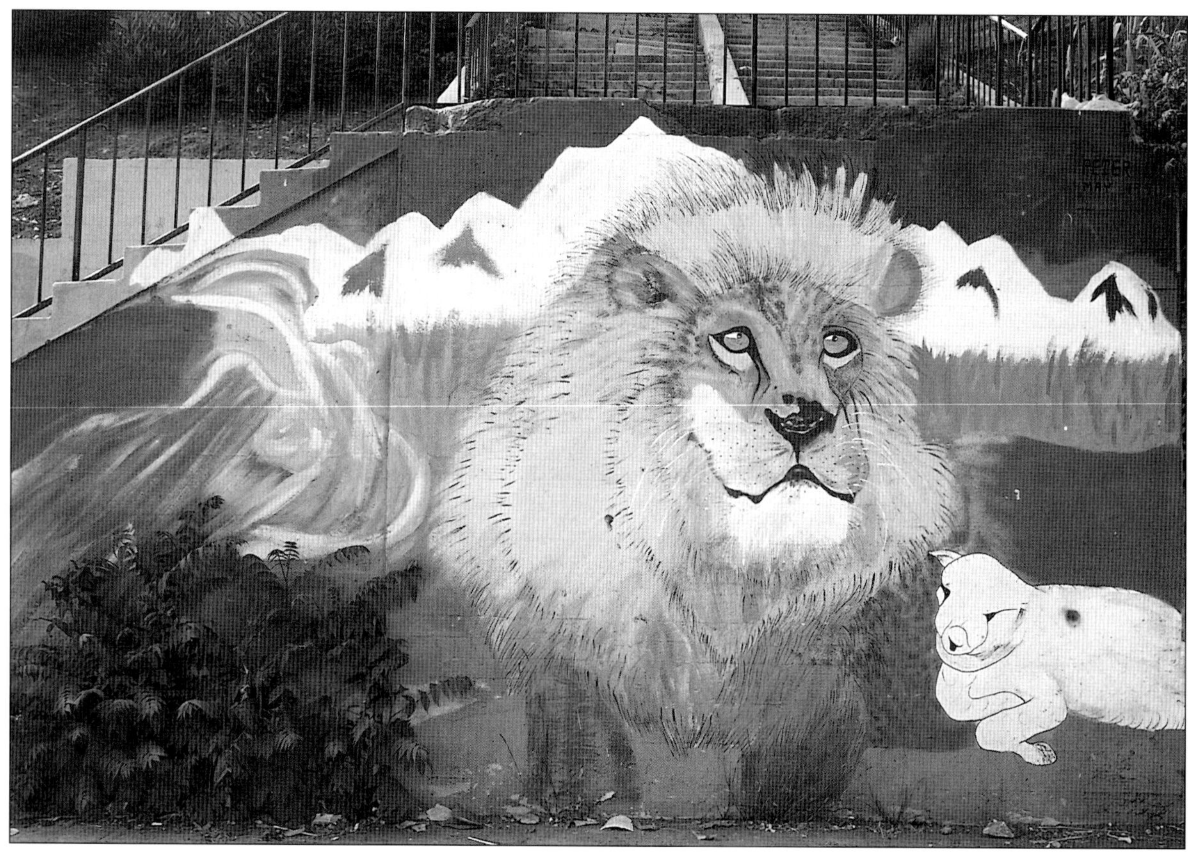

"Lion and Lamb" mural. The lamb was copied from a Jehovah's Witness pamphlet, but the lion was copied from a photograph in a wildlife calendar. Part of a series of images painted on Figueroa Street near Loreto Street in Highland Park.

guin holds its wings out to embrace a smaller one (plate 17).

A staple figure in Quezada's repertoire is the old cartoon character Betty Boop. Created for animated short films in the 1930s as a caricature of a flapper, Betty Boop experienced renewed popularity in the 1970s. Quezada has painted Betty Boop in a variety of incarnations—as Marilyn Monroe, as Elvira, as Santa Claus—on public walls as well as on sheets of wood and cardboard. He has an entire envelope full of postcards, photographs, and magazine clippings of different manifestations of Betty Boop. The character has become almost a trademark for Quezada, who, as he does with the animal images, has placed her in curious juxtapositions with an eclectic array of characters including lowriders, wizards, and pilgrims.

The Collage

Quezada does not draw or plan his murals on paper, although before he starts painting he has an idea in his head of how the different images will occupy the space on the wall relative to one another. He approaches the painting of a wall with a few preselected images, each of which he grids separately. His projects all proceed according to a general plan as well as having a certain degree of improvisation. Quezada explains that a particular surface of the wall or an empty spot may lend itself to the inclusion of a specific image, or extant images may suggest the inclusion of additional ones.

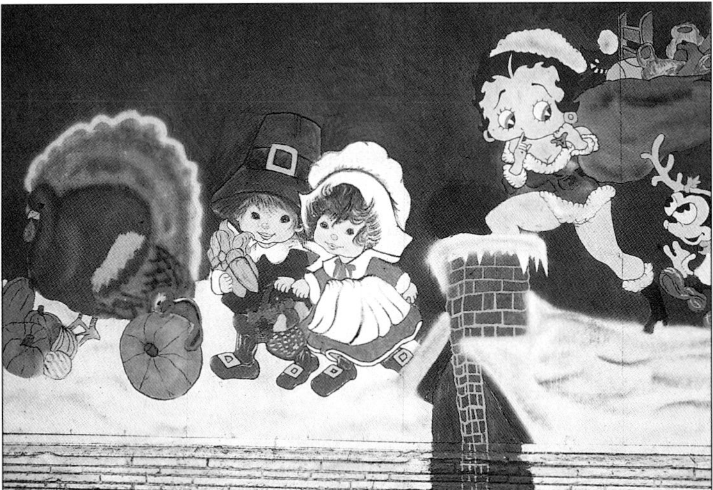

Part of a holiday mural painted in Highland Park in 1992.

Quezada's murals are configured according to a method that is best characterized as collage. He extracts his images from a broad array of sources. He is a visual and stylistic *bricoleur,* not subscribing to any one type of source material. In one mural, a *pachuco* character drawn from *Teen Angels* stands next to Jessica Rabbit from the movie *Who Framed Roger Rabbit?* In any given example, Quezada's scroll imagery and his lettering may have been derived from *Teen Angels,* existing graffiti in the vicinity, newspaper ads or mastheads, or graphics from product packaging. Furthermore, the way Quezada composes a single figure is often an act of mix-and-match. The face of a Jesus Christ painted in a recent mural was copied from

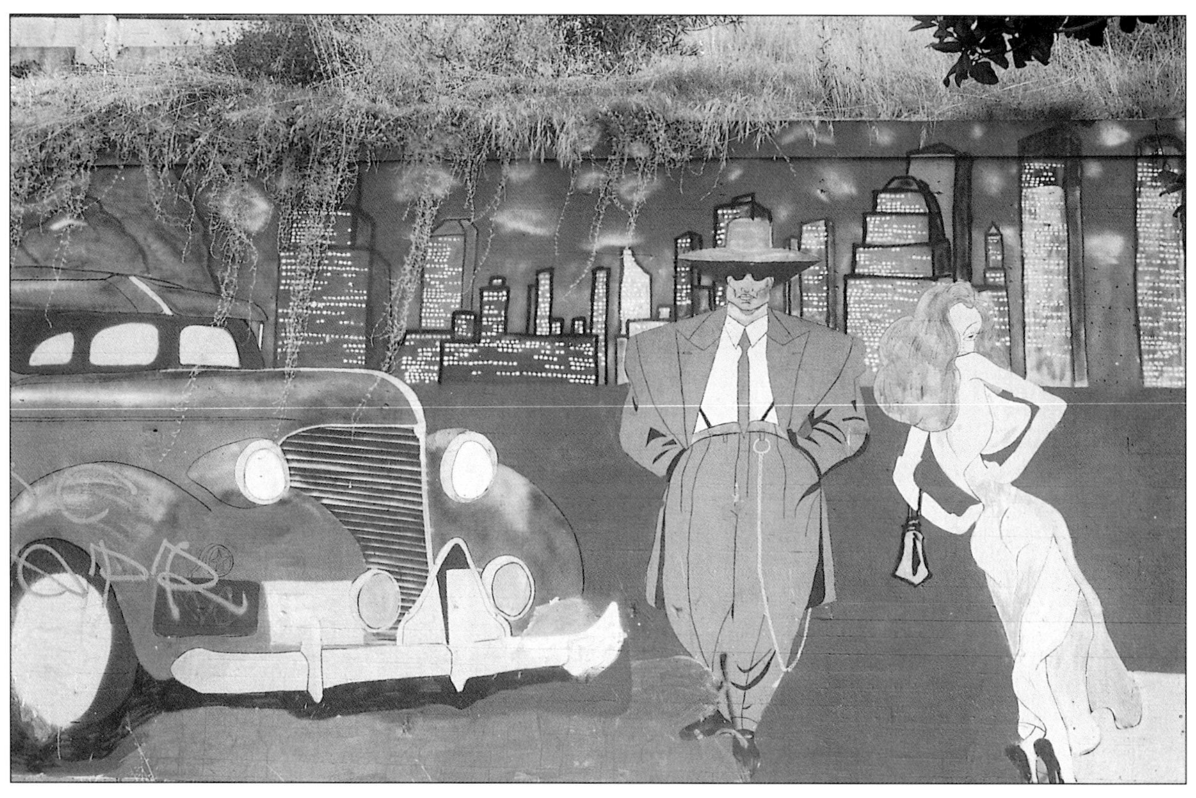

"Lion and Lamb" mural. Jessica Rabbit from the movie *Who Framed Roger Rabbit?* stands next to a zoot-suiter copied from the magazine *Teen Angels.*

a prayer card he purchased at a *mercado* (market); the body was modeled on a figure from the pamphlet of an indeterminate religious group. The head of the tiger in this same mural was copied from an advertisement while its body came from a tattoo (plate 17).

The way in which Quezada combines and positions images in his murals is also suggestive of collage. In some cases figures are integrated into a single scene. For instance, though different in style of execution, Jessica Rabbit and the *pachuco* character referred to above are painted so that they are proportionate to one another. They are standing on the same street with a night cityscape behind them.

In some murals, images cohere through a cautionary narrative warning of the wages of gang involvement. In these, the images may be presented in a chronological sequence across the wall. In 1988, Quezada and members of an area gang painted a mural that recounts the life of a gang member. The narrative unfolds from left to right on the wall, though scenes are not clearly differentiated and images are often layered in space, indicating multiple spatial and temporal planes (plate 4). The mural is composed of three main scenes. The first represents life on the street: a lamppost and vintage car serve as ambient props. A gangster character points a gun outward. In the next scene, a prison guard tower is flanked by the masks of tragedy and comedy. Cinder block walls topped with barbed wire project from either side. On the right side of the tower a man wearing a sad clown face bows his head down. A bespectacled judge floats slightly above and to the side of this figure. To the left of the tower, the bust of a young woman decked with roses looks toward the guard tower. The last scene is separated from the previous two by a fault line. A man, woman, and child stand next to a car in front of mountains. Rising out from behind the image of the car beside them is the figure of a zoot-suiter looking toward the center of the mural.

In 1992–93, Quezada painted a mural on the edge of Chinatown that consists of a panoply of over twenty images (plate 17). Though some may be grouped according to common subject, all of them have been applied to the wall as fragments of a general theme rather than as pieces of a single pictorial scene or linear narrative. Patches of different shades of blue and green constitute the background for most of the different images, ultimately linking and holding all of them together.

This particular mural was painted in the wake of the April 1992 civil unrest in Los Angeles. Quezada received a commission from the city to paint two murals that would represent the positive aspects of Los Angeles; hence the guiding message across the top of the mural: "Thru Good and Hard Times, L.A. Is Still #1." Among the images depicted beneath this message are Los Angeles landmarks and buildings, the logos of Los Angeles sports teams, and references to musical groups and famous persons.

The composition of this mural amounts to a geographic and social map of a small corner of Los Angeles configured from Quezada's position as he painted on the wall. The wall faces southeast and is oriented so that to the person in front of the mural, the left side points toward Chinatown; the right side extends northeasterly toward the Los Angeles River and in the general direction of the route to Quezada's neighborhood. Quezada painted motifs suggestive of Chinese culture or Chinatown on the left side of the wall: a tiger, a dragon, and a combat scene from a martial arts movie. On the right side of the wall a figure of Jesus Christ in a long flowing robe gestures with his arms eastward and stands above a family of three positioned behind a red Ford Fairlane. Quezada based the male figure in the mural on an old photograph of himself.

Various physical landmarks located in or just north of downtown Los Angeles are painted throughout the wall in rough approximation to their actual respective locations to one another: Dodger Stadium, the Griffith Park Observatory, the Los Angeles Zoo, the Hollywood sign, the Music Center, and a skyline of downtown Los Angeles, which Quezada painted using a photo and also by looking over his shoulder at the actual skyline. A portrait of James Dean was included in the mural not only as an allusion to the movie industry but also as a result of associative logic: the movie *Rebel without a Cause* was filmed on the grounds of the Griffith Park Observatory. A bust of James Dean now stands in front of the building, and, from that location, the Hollywood sign is visible. Los Angeles sports teams such as the Rams, the Kings, and the Raiders are represented. Quezada also refers to popular music indigenous to Los Angeles. The figure of a blond woman in a red dress is painted beneath the title of a song by The Doors, "L.A. Woman." Beneath this is the band's logotype and the lyrics to the song "Light My Fire." A madonna and child are painted adjacent to the figure of the woman. The Los Angeles punk scene of the 1970s and 1980s is represented in the mural by the band X and their song "Los Angeles." Quezada included in the mural the opening lines of this song—"She had to leave Los Angeles . . ."—and indicates that this song more realistically expresses what it is like to live in Los Angeles than the cheery superficiality of Randy Newman's "I Love L.A." Exercising artistic license, Quezada chose the mohawked figure of Annabella Lwin, a British singer, to represent visually the Los Angeles punk scene.

In other murals, it is only adjacency that links images together, as neither back-

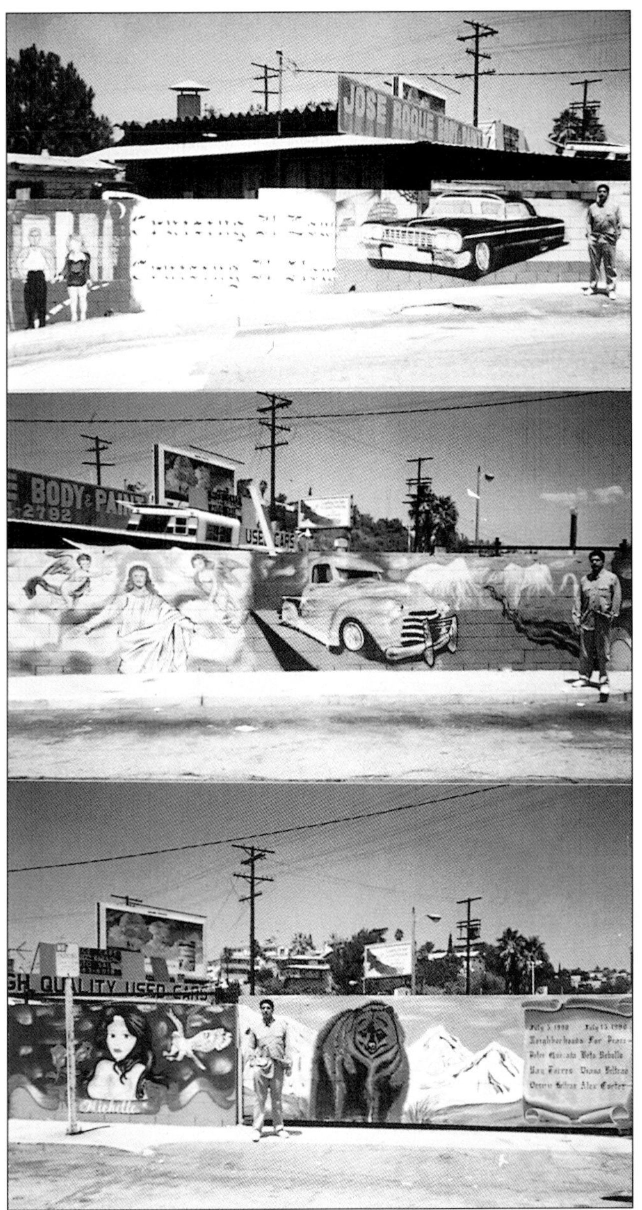

Jose Roque Auto Body and Paint in Silver Lake on Sunset Blvd. and Ellett Place. The length of the entire piece is approximately ninety feet.

ground nor narrative provides a sense of continuity. One of the murals with which Quezada is most satisfied is a series of discretely framed and distinct scenes painted along the low retaining wall of Jose Roque Auto Body Repair in Silver Lake. The images include a man and woman standing against a night cityscape; Old English letters spelling out "Cruising It Low, Cruising It Slow"; a blue car; a figure of Christ flanked by two angels; a Chevy panel truck; a picture of a woman whose bust is crossed by a ribbon that reads "Michelle," the name of Quezada's wife; and a bear (what Quezada calls a "G.P." or "general purpose" bear). A mile or so down the road from Jose Roque are three connecting city-owned walls on which Quezada has painted the L.A. Dodgers pitcher Orel Hersheiser, a muscular superhero character ("The Punisher"), and the message written in cursive: "Try to Express Yourself Artistically, Not Destructively."

Quezada has an eclectic visual sensibility that enables him to draw upon established and culturally loaded images such as Guadalupe and *pachucos,* as well as unicorns, cartoon characters, and sentimental drawings of animals. Part of this has to do with his audience. Ever attentive to those who live amid the walls where he paints, he consults and enlists the assistance and suggestions of those who pass by to watch and talk to him while he works. During the summer of 1994, Quezada spent over a month in one alley of El Sereno painting the garages and cinder block walls of private residences. He had initially been disappointed by the indifference of residents to the upkeep of their alley, and he had decided to finish quickly the piece he had started and return to surface streets to paint. Eventually, neighbors came out to talk with him, and several local youths became involved in the painting. Quezada ended up painting five to six additional pieces, including, at the request of some of the younger children, Barney the purple dinosaur and the Mighty Morphin Power Rangers.

Quezada's collection of source material and his process of compilation have much in common with the aesthetic sensibility that anthropologists, art historians, and folklorists have ascribed to the creators of pop art, surrealism, quilts, and home altars. The terms "pastiche" and "bricolage" are often used to describe these projects. The quality identified in all of these instances is the insight that inspires someone to recycle images or objects and to juxtapose genres, materials, and subjects not immediately associated with each other, so that the person (consciously or unconsciously) breaks down the distinctions in art between mass and personal; high and low; old and new. Art historian Tomás Ybarra-Frausto has discussed a similar attitude or taste in Chicano vernacular expression as

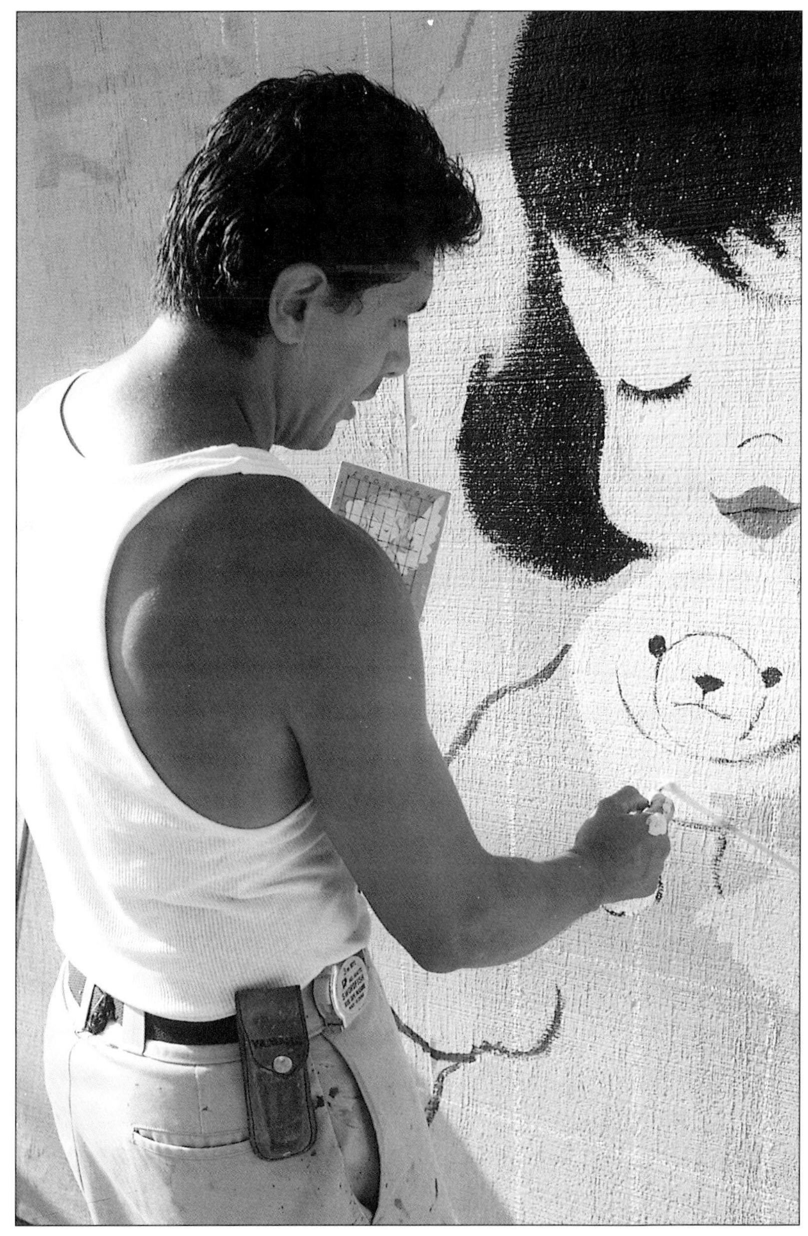

Mural for Peter's daughter Melissa "Titi" is painted on a garage. The piece is one of several that he painted along an alley in El Sereno during the summer of 1994. The figure of the girl is rendered as his daughter, but it was copied from a greeting card of an angel holding a lamb. Peter cut out the wings, painted the figure's hair black, and put a seal (his daughter's favorite toy) in her arms instead of a lamb.

rasquachismo. He describes *rasquachismo* as a working-class sensibility born of necessity. He writes: "*Rasquachismo* is a compendium of all the *movidas* deployed in immediate, day-to-day living. Resilience and resourcefulness spring from making do with what is at hand (*hacer rendir las cosas*). This use of available resources engenders hybridization, juxtaposition, and integration. *Rasquachismo* is a sensibility attuned to mixtures and confluence, preferring communion over purity" (156).

Quezada's use of divergent sources and his incorporation of different styles and genres of representation certainly resonate with *rasquachismo*. But more generally, his process of creation attests to the fact that people living in postindustrial, mass-mediated society are not solely consumers but are recyclers and translators of these materials from one context and medium to another. Categories of high versus low are disregarded in such translations; for his murals, Quezada consults and compares reproductions of classical art, comic book imagery, movie posters, and the penciled images drawn by a prisoner on handkerchiefs (*paños*). What's more, means of production may involve "low tech" and "high tech" procedures and techniques. For instance, Quezada bases the images in his murals not only on found objects but also on photographs that he purposefully takes. He once requested that a friend of his print in reverse a photograph he had taken so that the image would be oriented in the proper direction for a mural he was painting.

People can be genuinely moved, captivated, and inspired by different genres, styles, and media. The use of a song sung by Elvis Presley and the image of Jessica Rabbit in a mural discussing gang violence is vibrant testimony to the cacophony that provides much of the raw material for contemporary folk and popular expressions and to the personal and serendipitous uses individuals make of their visual environment.

The Memory/The Impression

Graffiti and murals implicitly and explicitly record public and personal events and messages. Gang members write on walls the names of those who have died; Peter Quezada has painted murals commemorating or dedicated to dead friends and acquaintances.

In fact, the first mural Quezada painted on a surface street was commemorative. In 1988, on the twentieth anniversary of the assassination of Robert Kennedy, Quezada painted a portrait of Kennedy beneath the inscription: "In Loving Memory of Robert F. Kennedy. God Bless." He later did a similar piece to mark the twenty-fifth anniversary of the assassination of John F. Kennedy (plate 3).

Many of Quezada's other murals record dates and events significant to Los Angelenos. His murals have announced the victories of Los Angeles sports teams, the

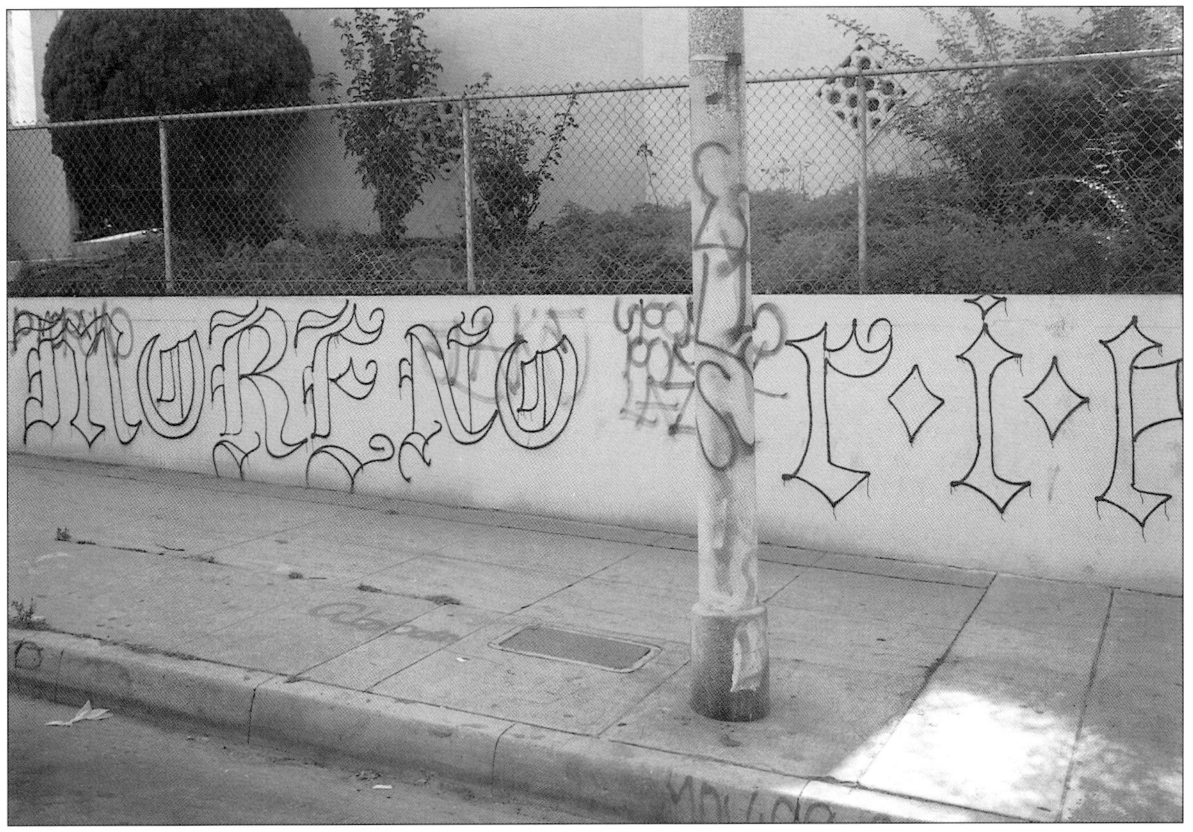

Commemorative graffiti in
Lincoln Heights.

departures of hometown heroes, and the spate of disasters that have recently struck the city:

•L.A. Lakers World Champions
•L.A. Dodgers World Champions
•Adios Fernando, Good Luck Homeboy [former Los Angeles Dodgers pitcher, Fernando Valenzuela]
•Though Shakin', Bakin', and Quakin' L.A.'s Still #1

The walls that Quezada paints engender an act of memory in another way as well. There are other artists who, like Quezada, independently paint on walls in northeast Los Angeles. Each artist works in a distinctive style and with a different agenda, but forms and images painted by one individual are appreciated, influenced, or replaced by others.

In the early 1980s, Quezada admired the work of an artist who painted religious imagery on the walls of the Arroyo Seco and signed his pieces St. Roché. Quezada had long wondered to whom the work belonged, and, when they began to wear away from age and graffiti, he wanted to touch them up. He later learned that St. Roché had been killed in the early 1980s. In 1990, Quezada dedicated his "Lion and the Lamb/Peace in the Valley" mural to St. Roché, a person whom he knew only through a series of paintings that no longer existed except in his memory. The inscription for the mural reads: "This mural is dedicated to a wonderful young person who, when the Lord called upon him, responded. Here's missing you. Jerome 'Jerry' Roché 'AKA' St. Roché 4–19–58 12–28–84 God Rest."

Though St. Roché mainly worked on the walls of the Arroyo Seco, Quezada paid homage to these works not at the site of their creation but on the wall of a major surface street. Similarly, Quezada's murals have traveled beyond the physical walls on which they are painted via the impression they have made on other people. His murals have appeared in local newspapers about a dozen times, both with and without accompanying articles. I recently watched a music video by a local Chicano Elvis Presley impersonator who calls himself El Vez. A mural of Quezada's is repeatedly used as the backdrop for an adaptation of "In the Ghetto" sung by El Vez as "In el Barrio." While at a photocopy shop waiting for copies to be made of the manuscript for this monograph, I was perusing the wall next to the cash register on which the proprietors have hung reproductions of some of the artwork that has been duplicated at their business. I noticed a photograph of a mural of Jesus Christ that Quezada painted on the side of the Highland Park Theatre. The photographer had tilted the camera almost to a diagonal. He/she might have been shooting the mural as a backdrop to the young boy run-

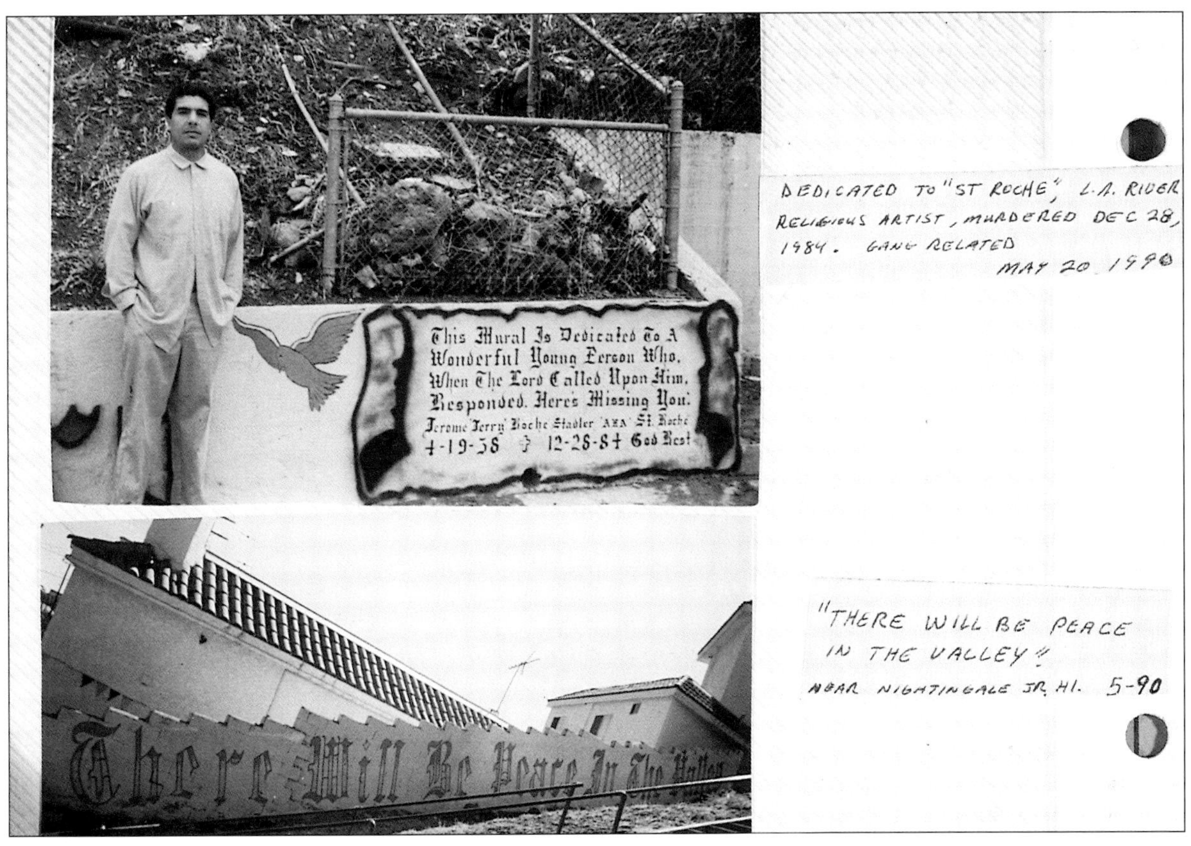

From the pages of Peter's photo albums. He dedicated the "Lion and Lamb" mural to St. Roché, a graffiti artist who was killed in 1984.

ning through the frame or shooting the mural when the child ran past. Interestingly, the mural no longer exists as it appears in this photograph. A graffiti artist who calls himself Zender reworked Quezada's figure, changing the style of the original image that now lies somewhere underneath (plates 14, 15).

The images and words painted on public walls are absorbed, interpreted, erased, and superceded. Quezada has managed to keep a record of the marks he has made on the landscape. He keeps several three-ring binders that serve as photo albums. Most of the pictures in these binders record the walls he has painted with "before" and "after" shots (plate 3). This record began in 1980 when he was whitewashing the wall of the Highland Park Furniture Store. The owner of the store suggested to his neighbor, the owner of a photography studio, that he photograph the wall before and after its make-over. Quezada now continues his own meticulous documentation process. Pieces of masking tape or Post-it notes have been carefully cut and adhered to the different photos, and he has written notes about the images, such as:

- Ave 56 and Baltimore Street Highland Park Dec. 20, 1990.
- '62 Chevy Impala 23rd St. and Harvard Central L.A. 2-89
- "Before" Picture Highland Theatre 56 and Figueroa, Highld Pk 7-29-88
- "After" Picture Highland Theatre 56 and Figueroa, HL'P 7–29–88

One of Quezada's albums is labeled "Gangs" and contains photographs of friends and people he has worked with formally at CYGS or informally through his mural painting. Black and blue ink on the masking tape or Post-it notes describe the photos. In red, or sometimes purple, Quezada has added, where necessary, "R.I.P." and the date of death. Gang members often come to Quezada looking for photographs of their friends who have died, as he is sometimes the only source for their visual memory. Quezada also keeps in this album a napkin that bears doodled images, a gang moniker, and signatures sketched in felt-tip pen by him and four of his friends one afternoon as they sat in a restaurant. Post-it notes attached to the napkin indicate that he is the only one still alive. As is the case with his murals, Quezada acknowledges the precariousness of life for those involved with gangs. He associates many of his murals with people who have been killed, either explictly through commemoration or because those who participated in the painting have since died.

Quezada's photo albums are the safekeepers of experience. The people and murals they document are detached from physical existence and are therefore preserved from the aging, damage, and extinction to which they might otherwise be subjected on the street. The photographs are distillations of actual experiences, people, and places, and they can enact the project of remembering. The records of Quezada's work made by other people are not necessarily informed by the same personal impulse to remember. But these images, like Quezada's tribute to St. Roché, are examples of how markings on the wall—murals and even graffiti—can, despite their ephemeral imprint on concrete, leave powerful impressions upon the imagination.

References

Castleman, Craig. 1982. *Getting Up: Subway Graffiti in New York.* Cambridge, Mass.: The Massachusetts Institute of Technology Press.

Cesaretti, Gusmano. 1975. *Street Writers: A Guided Tour of Chicano Graffiti.* Los Angeles: Acrobat Books.

Cockcroft, Eva, John Weber, and Jim Cockcroft. 1977. *Toward a People's Art: The Contemporary Mural Movement.* New York: E.P. Dutton & Co., Inc.

Colvin, Richard Lee. 1993. "Taggers Debate Their Critics Who See No Art in Graffiti." *Los Angeles Times* (9/1/93): B1.

Cook, Lynn. 1990. "The Independent Group: British and American Pop Art, A 'Palimpcestuous' Legacy." In *Modern Art and Popular Culture: Readings in High and Low,* eds. Kirk Varnedoe and Adam Gopnik. New York: Harry N. Abrams, Inc.

Downs, Anthony. 1981. *Neighborhoods and Urban Development.* Washington, D.C.: The Brookings Institute.

Gray, Nicolete. 1974. "Lettering and Society." *Visible Language* 8 (3): 250.

——. 1986. *A History of Lettering: Creative Experiment and Letter Identity.* Boston: David R. Godine.

Herbert, Ray. 1985. "LA—A City Divided and Proud of It." *Los Angeles Times* (12/9/85): Pt. 1, 1.

Mazón, Mauricio. 1984. *The Zoot-Suit Riots: A Psychology of Symbolic Annihilation.* Austin, Tex.: University of Texas Press.

Merken, Betty and Stefan. 1987. *Wall Art: Megamurals and Supergraphics.* Philadelphia: Running Press.

Mesa-Bains, Amalia. 1990. "Chicano Bodily Aesthetics." In catalog for the exhibition *Body/Culture: Chicano Figuration.* Exhibition curated by Richard J. Kubiak and Elizabeth Partch. Catalog edited by Elizabeth Partch. Rohmert Park, Cal.: Sonoma State University.

Plascencia, Luis F.B. 1983. "Low Riding in the Southwest: Cultural Symbols in the Mexican Community." In *History, Culture and Society: Chicano Studies in the 1980s,* ed. Mario T. García, et al., 141-175. Ypsilanti, MI: Bilingual Press Review.

Romotsky, Jerry and Sally R. 1976. *Los Angeles Barrio Calligraphy.* Los Angeles: Dawson's Book Shop.

Ryden, Kent C. 1993. *Mapping the Invisible Landscape: Folklore, Writing, and the Sense of Place.* Iowa City: University of Iowa Press.

Sánchez-Tranquilino, Marcos. 1991. *"Mi Casa No Es Su Casa:* Chicano Murals and Barrio Calligraphy as Systems of Signification at Estrada Courts 1972–1978." Master's thesis, University of California, Los Angeles.

Seriff, Suzanne and José Limon. 1986. "Bits and Pieces: The Mexican American Folk Aesthetic." In *Art Among Us, Arte Entre Nosotros: Mexican American Folk Art of San Antonio,* eds. Pat Jasper and Kay Turner, 40–49. San Antonio: San Antonio Museum Association.

Soja, Edward W. 1989. *Postmodern Geographies: The Reassertion of Space in Critical Social Theory.* London and England: Verso.

Sommer, Robert. 1975. *Street Art.* New York: Quick Fox.

Sorell, Victor Alejandro. 1990. "Words and Images in the Margin: Chicano Visual Art and the Canon." In catalog for the exhibition *Body/Culture: Chicano Figuration.* Exhibition curated by Richard J. Kubiak and Elizabeth Partch. Catalog edited by Elizabeth Partch. Rohmert Park, Cal.: Sonoma State University.

Stewart, Susan. 1987. "*Ceci Tuera Cela:* Graffiti as Crime and Art." In *Life After Postmodernism: Essays on Value and Culture,* ed. John Fekete. New York: St. Martin's Press.

Stone, Michael Cutler. 1990. "*Bajito y Suavecito* [Low and Slow]: Low Riding and the 'Class' of Class." In *Studies in Latin American Popular Culture* 9: 85–126.

Ybarra-Frausto, Tomás. 1990. "Arte Chicano: Images of a Community." In *Signs from the Heart: California Chicano Murals,* eds. Eva Sperling Cockcroft and Holly Barnet Sánchez. Venice, Cal.: Social and Public Arts Resource Center (SPARC).

——.1990. "Rasquachismo: A Chicano Sensibility." In *Chicano Art: Resistance and Affirmation,* 1965–1985, eds. Richard Griswold del Castillo, Teresa McKenna, and Yvonne Yarbro-Bejarano. Los Angeles: Wight Art Gallery, UCLA.

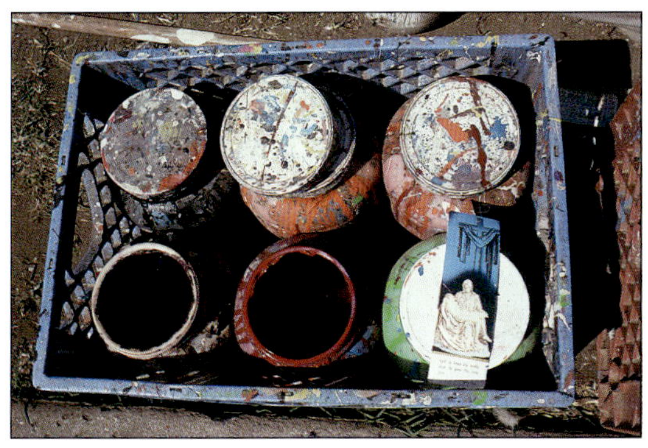

PLATE 1

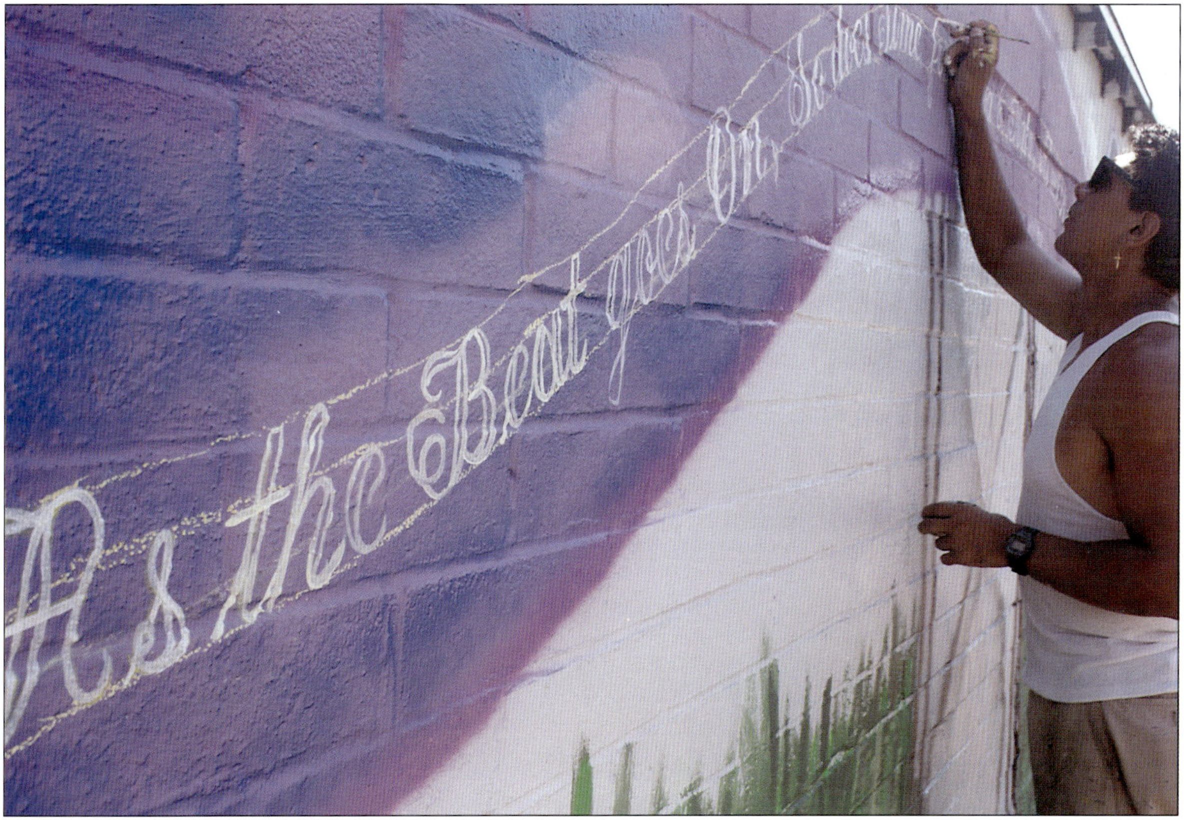

PLATE 2
Peter paints the lettering with a brush. This is part of a mural that depicts themes from the Disney movie *The Lion King.* Peter painted the mural in an alley in El Sereno during the summer of 1994 for his son. *Monterey Avenue/Huntington Drive*

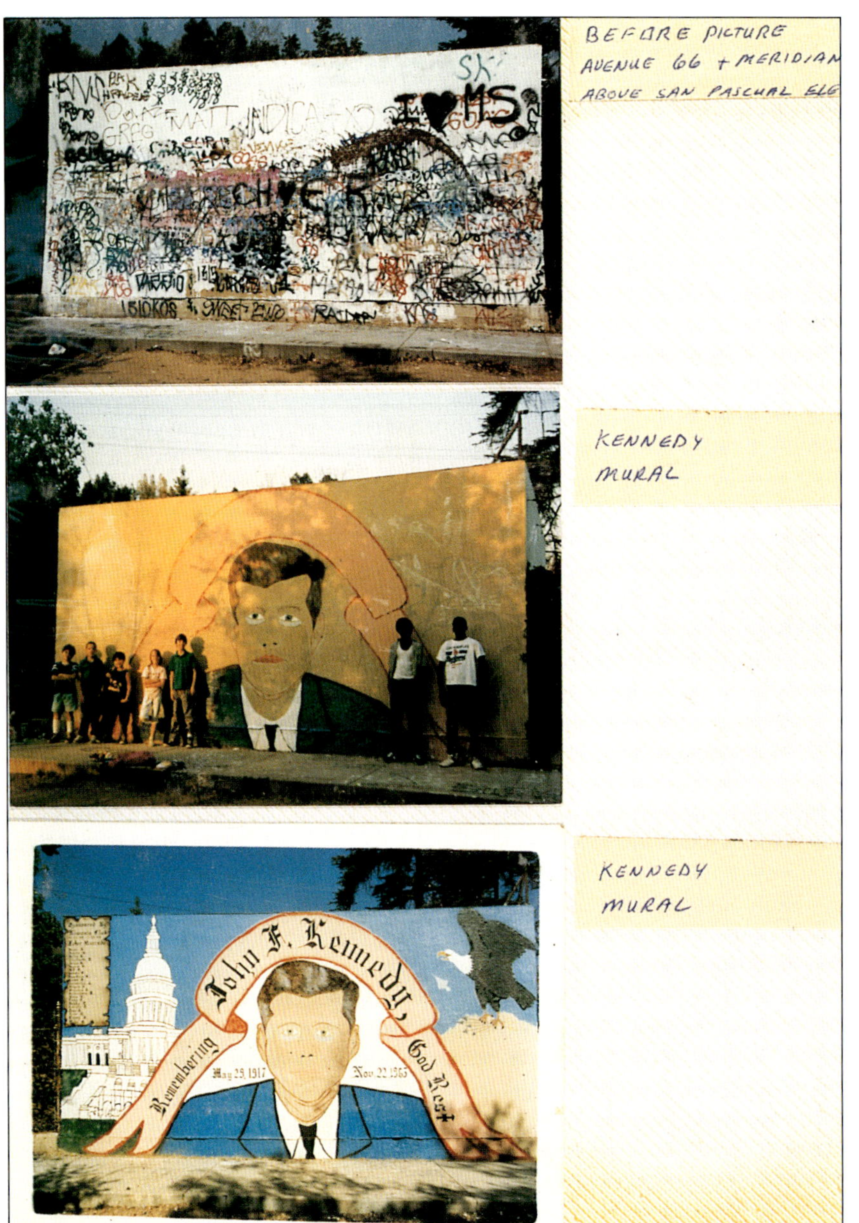

PLATE 3
Peter's documentation of the process of painting a mural on the twenty-fifth anniversary of the assassination of John F. Kennedy, no longer extant. *Avenue 64/ Meridian Street*

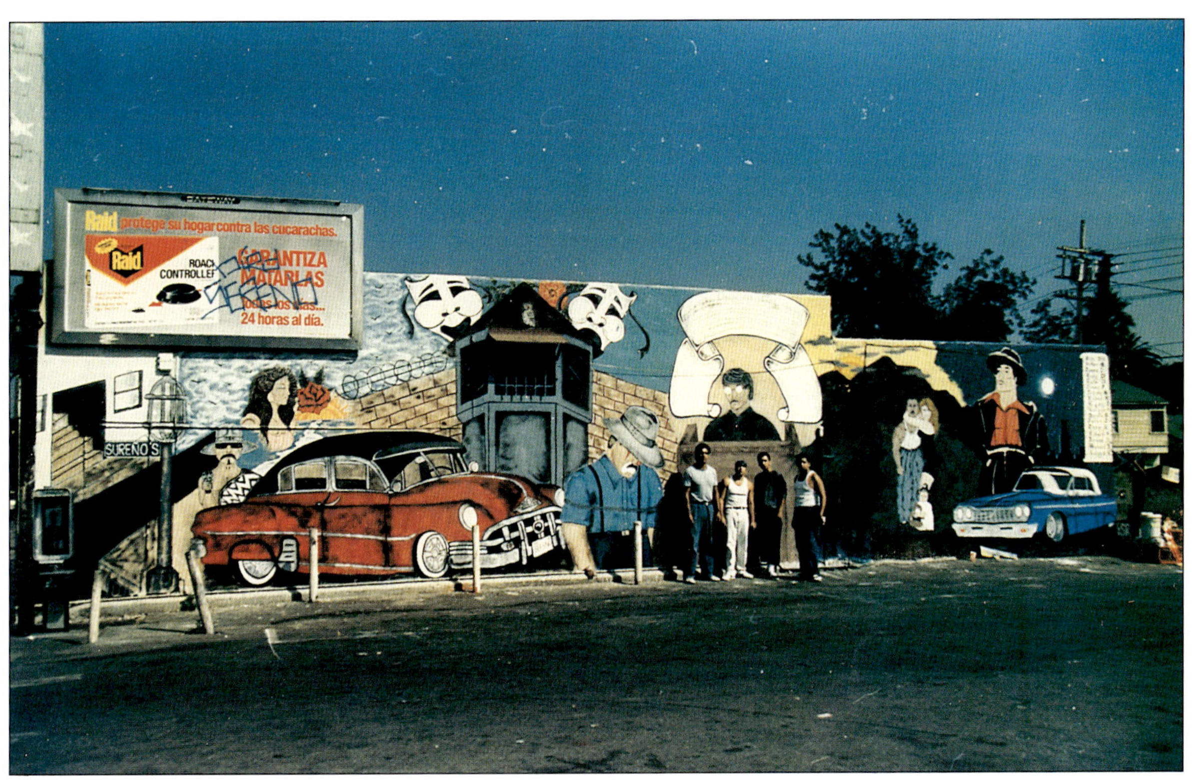

PLATE 4
Mural painted with members of an El Sereno gang. Peter copied the zoot-suiter character on the far right from a photo he took of the poster for the film *Zoot Suit.* In the original image, the figure looks to the left. Quezada wanted to paint it facing to the right—inward towards the mural. A friend of his who owns a photography studio reversed the negative. No longer extant.
Huntington Drive/Van Horne Avenue

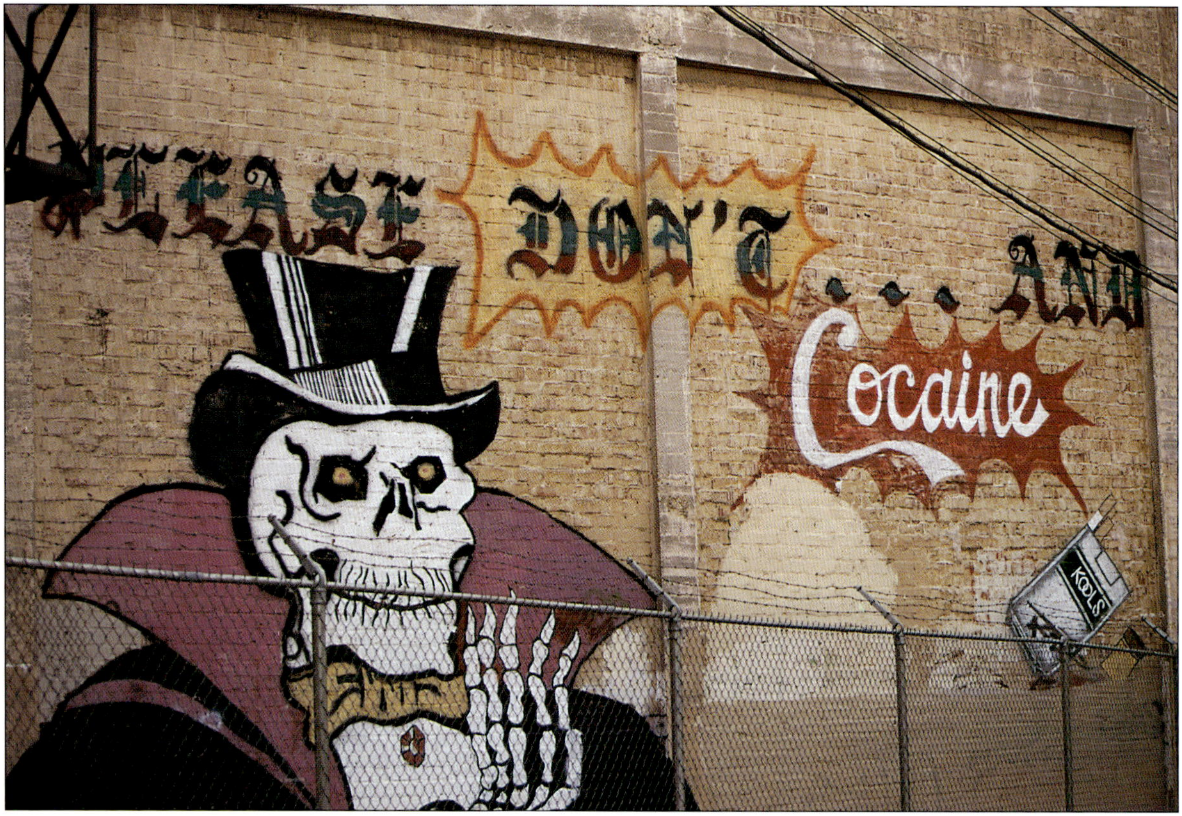

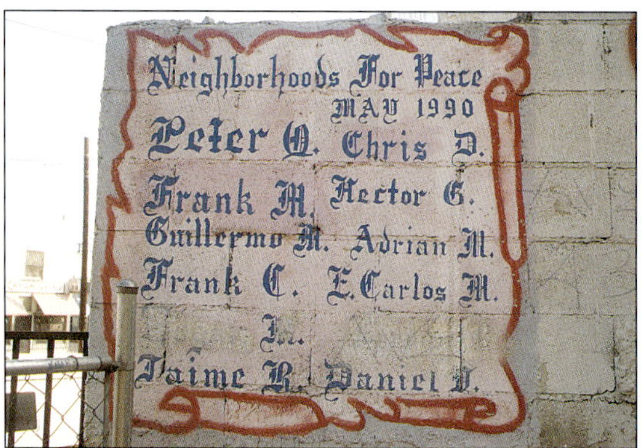

PLATE 5
Mural painted in an alley in El Sereno. This initially included a figure of the Zig Zag man. *Eastern Avenue/ Huntington Drive*

PLATE 6
"Roll call" or "honor roll" listing those who assisted in the murals. Peter paints the names against the motif of a scroll. From the "Peace in the Valley" mural. *Figueroa Street and Loreto Street*

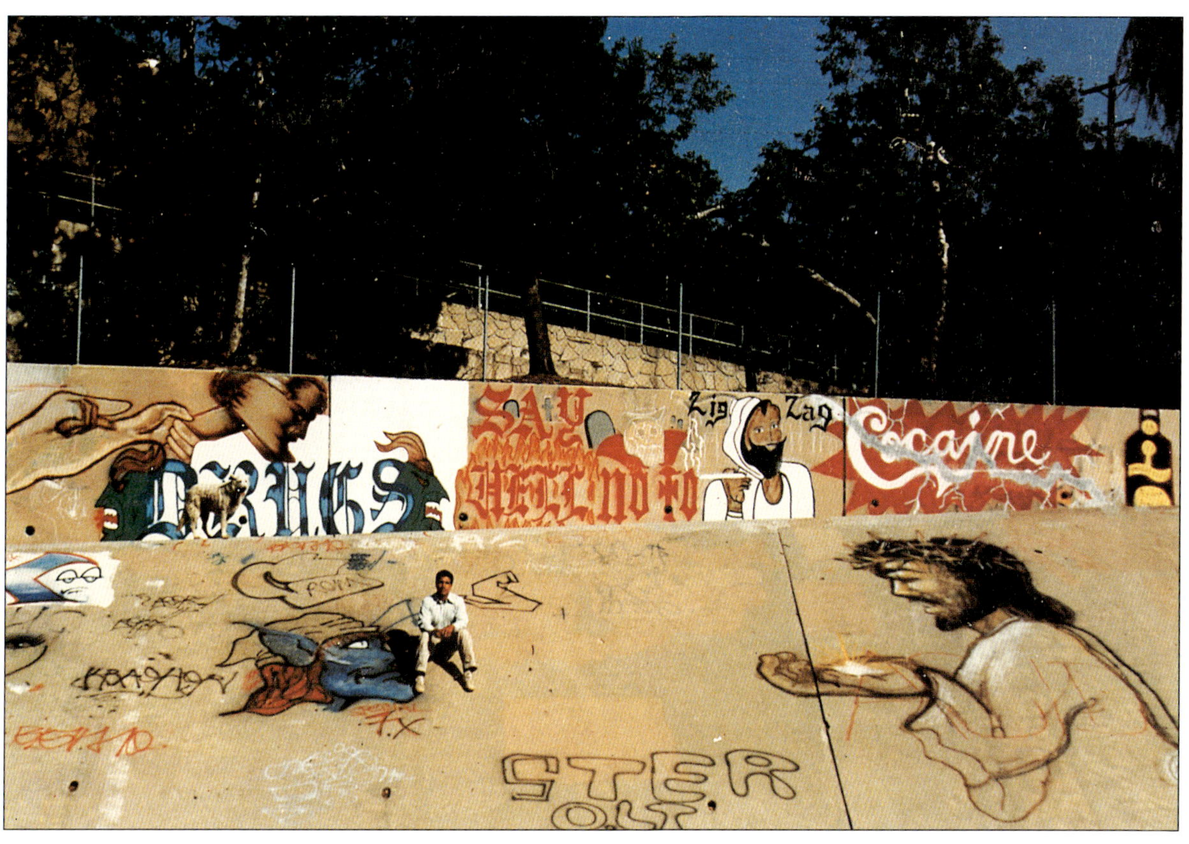

PLATE 7
This photograph was taken in 1988. The character next to the word "Cocaine," written to resemble the Coca-Cola logotype, is the Zig Zag man whose image is used in the packaging for Zig Zag cigarette papers.
Arroyo Seco between Avenue 43 and Avenue 52

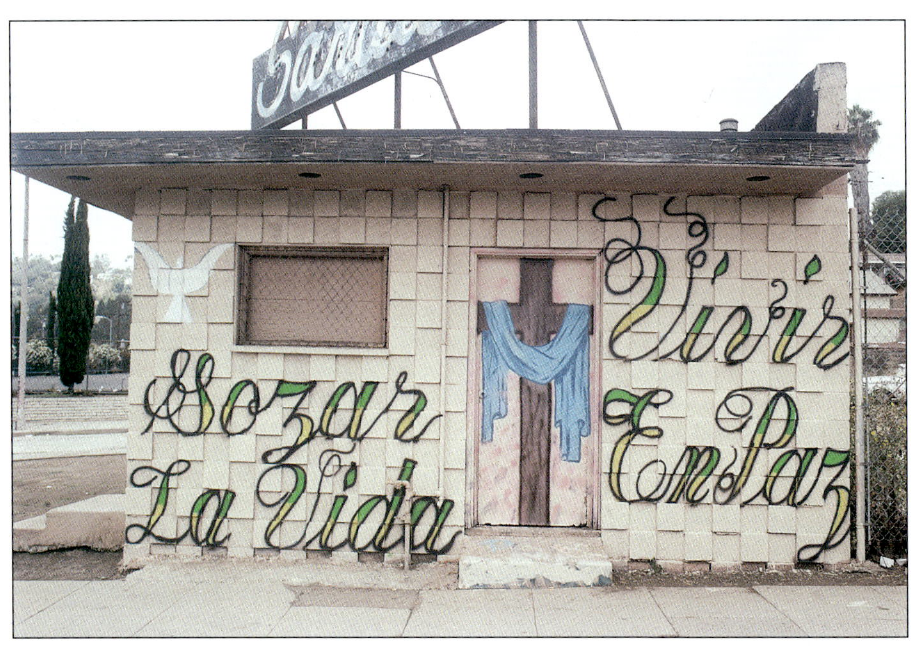

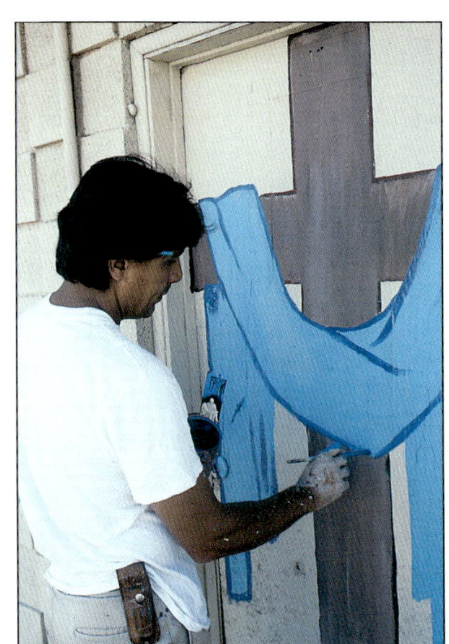

PLATE 8
"Enjoy life"; "Live in Peace." Painted in El Sereno on an abandoned bar. *Monterey Road/Huntington Drive*

PLATE 9
The image of the cross draped with a swath of blue fabric is modeled after the image on a bookmark.

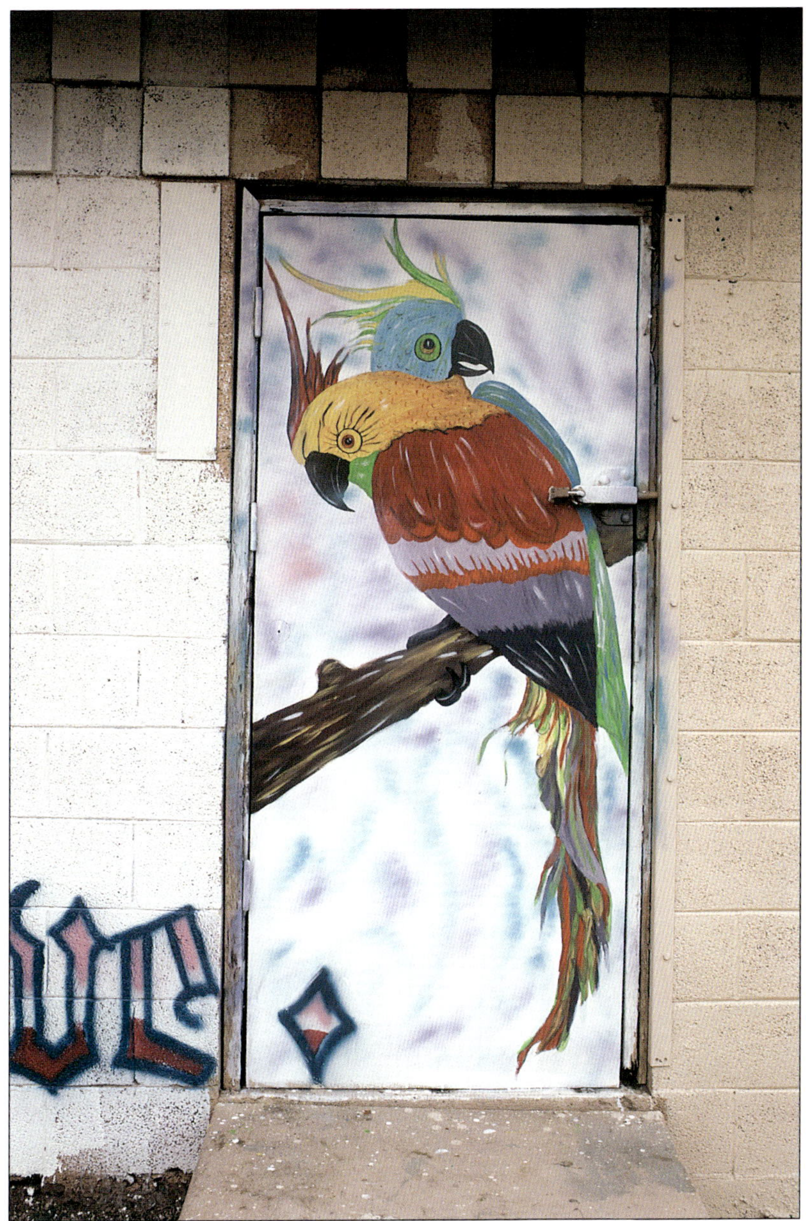

PLATE 10
Another wall of the same building in plates 9 and 10. This image was painted next to the message: "Peace Brothers, It's Thee Only Way If We're To Survive."

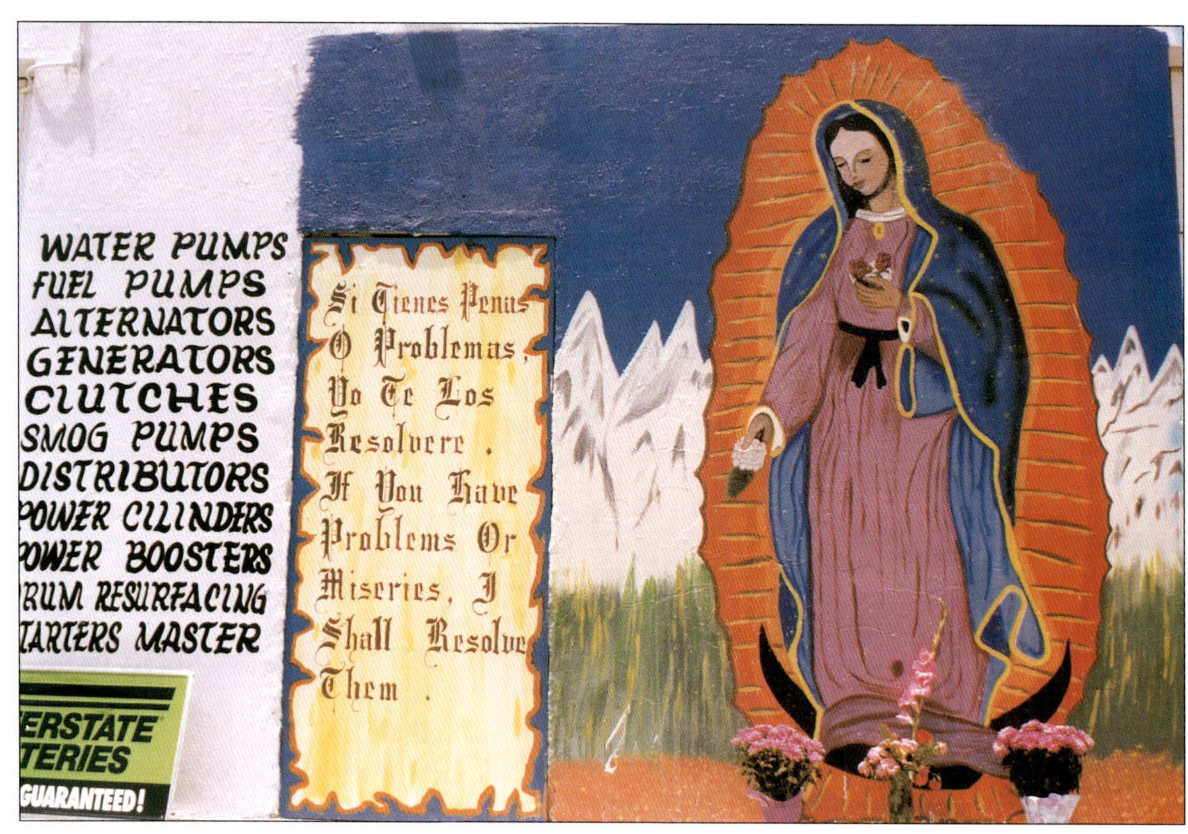

PLATE 11
Virgen de Guadalupe painted on the exterior wall of an auto repair shop in El Sereno. The mural was defaced three times. This photograph was taken after the second time. *Maycrest Avenue/Huntington Drive*

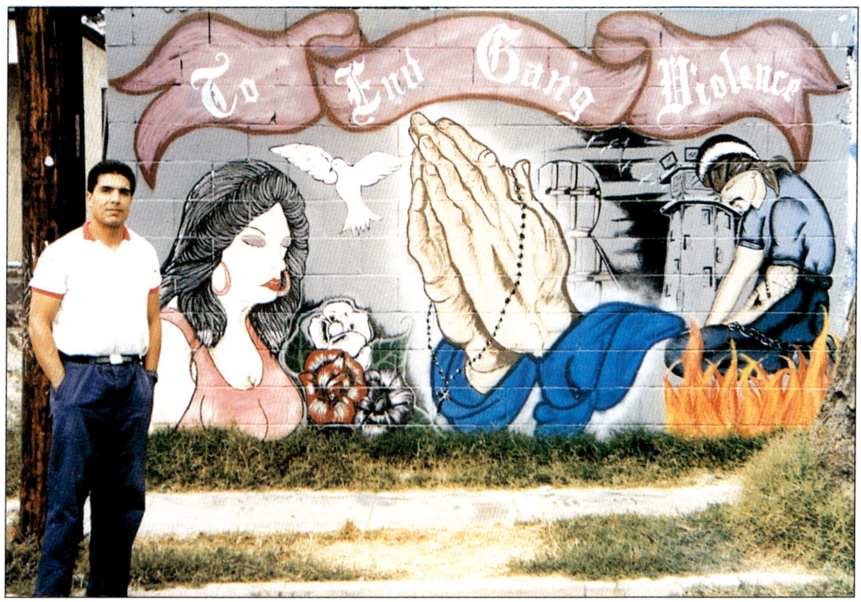

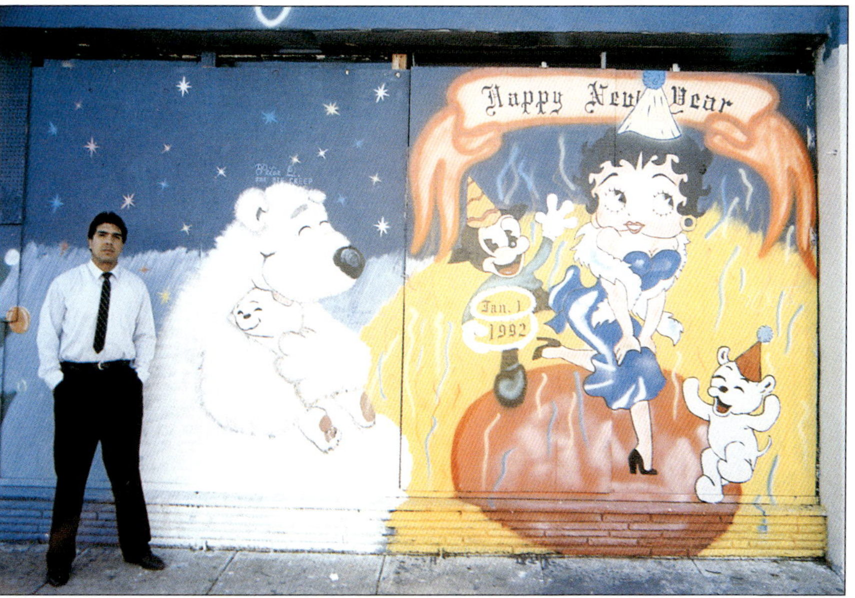

PLATE 12
"Pray to End Gang Violence." *Esmeralda Street/ Huntington Drive*

PLATE 13
Part of a holiday mural painted in 1992 with the assistance of members of the local Kiwanis Club, Soledad Enrichment Action, his friend Stretch, and his son. Peter has painted the big bear as himself and the small one as his son Peter-Bryan. Many of the murals he now paints he does for the enjoyment of his son and daughter, Melissa. *Figueroa Street/Avenue 53*

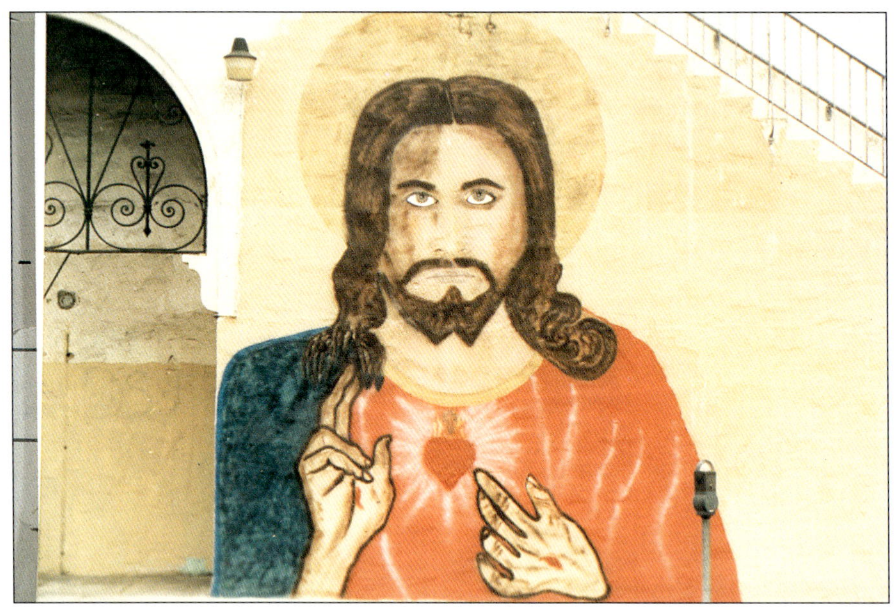

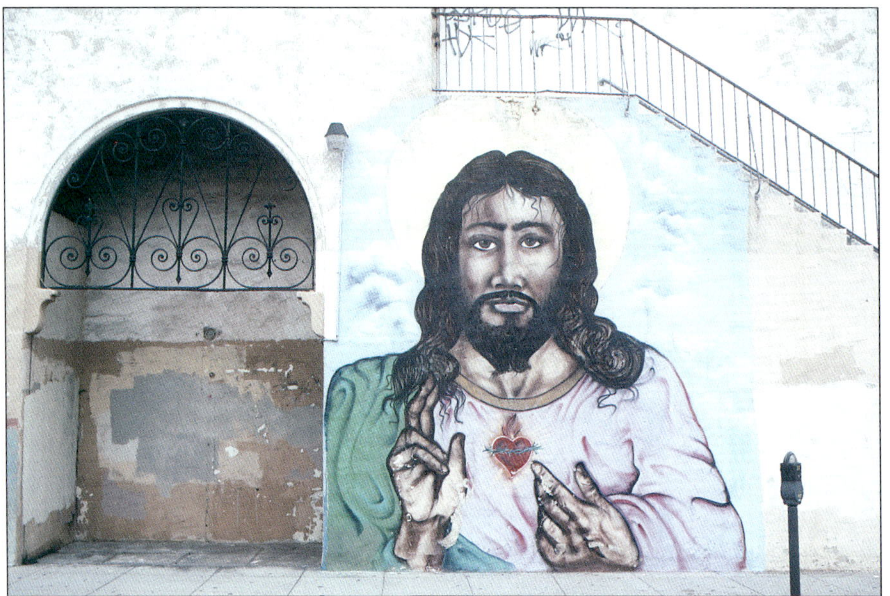

PLATE 14
Peter painted this figure of Jesus Christ on the side of a Highland Park movie theatre in 1988. *Avenue 56/Figueroa Street*

PLATE 15
An area graffiti artist who calls himself Zender recently reworked the Jesus Christ figure.

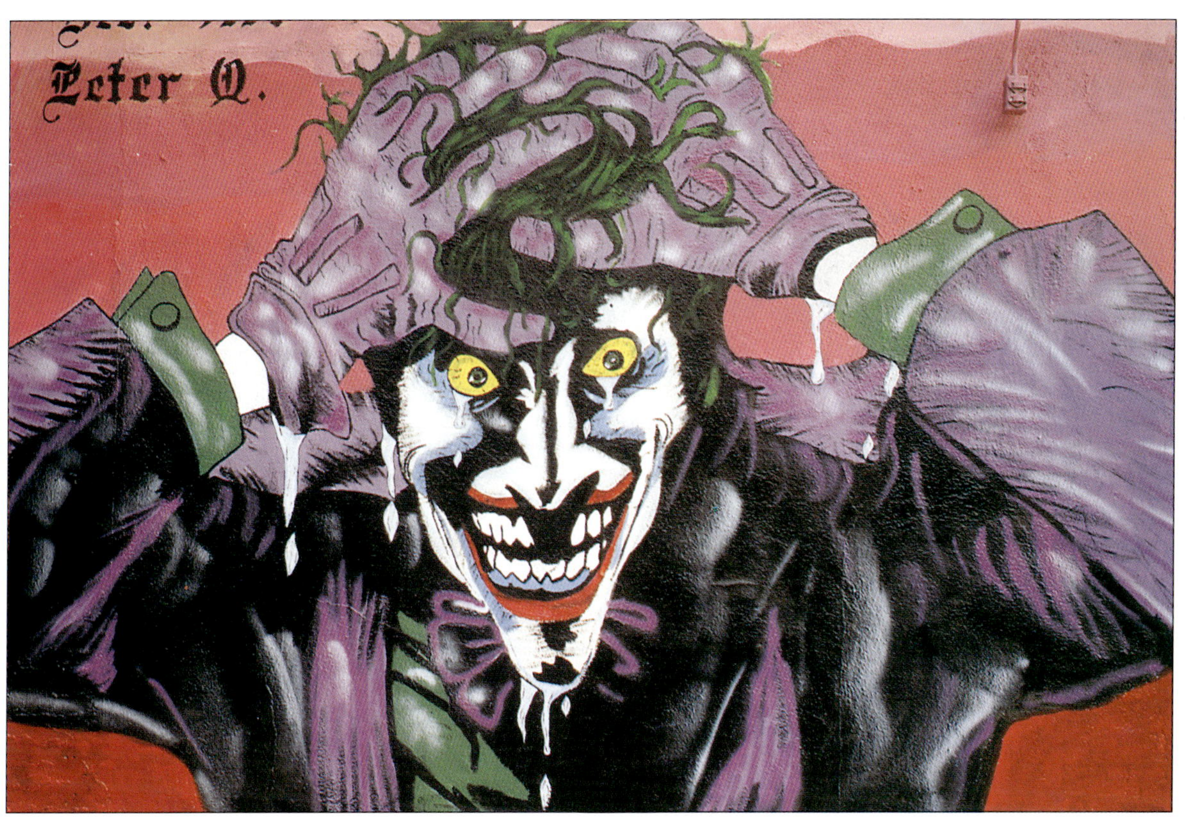

PLATE 16
This mural was painted across from a junior high school. The message above the image states: "Hey, No Joking. Stay in School." This is the second mural Peter has painted using the character of the Joker. The first time he used the image with the message "End The Insanity: Have the Courage to Say No To Gangs."
Eastern Avenue/Lynnfield

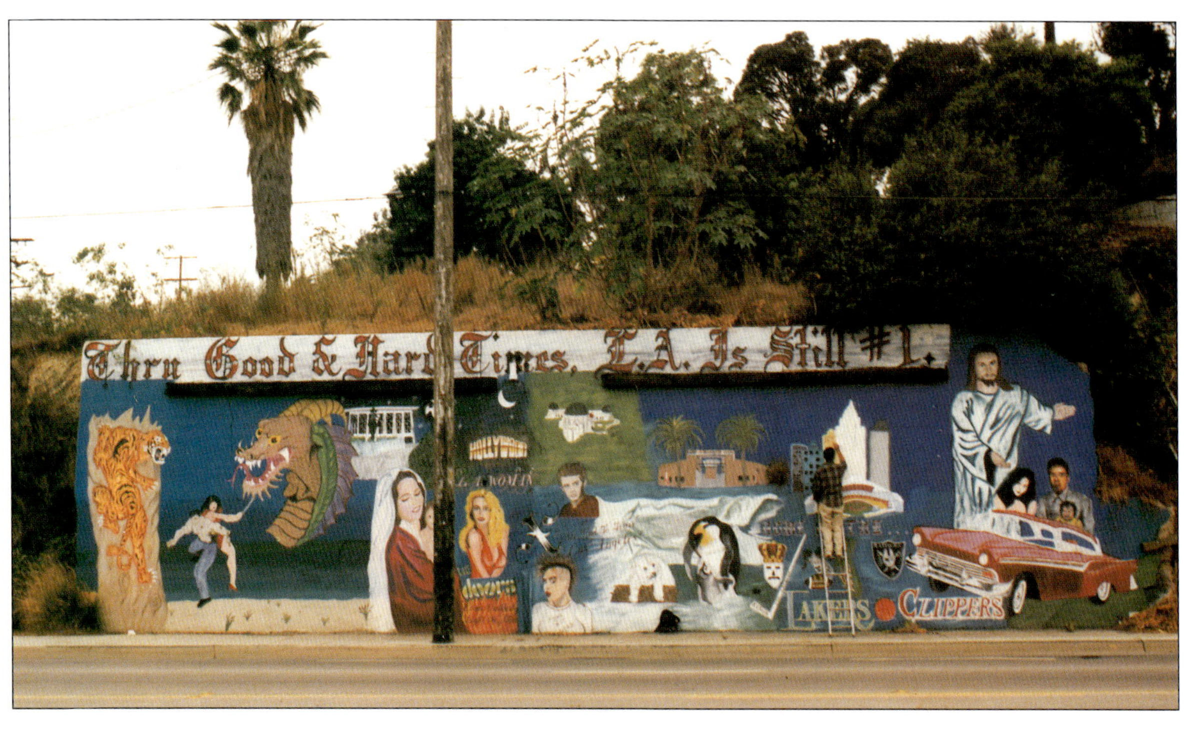

PLATE 17
This mural, located on the eastern edge of Chinatown, was commissioned by the city in the wake of the 1992 civil unrest that followed the acquittal of the officers who had beaten Rodney King. The penguin characters in the bottom center were copied from an advertisement for a decorative plate edition. As with the bears in the mural in plate 13, the large penguin and small penguin represent Peter and his son. *Broadway just west of the L.A. River*